The Well
of
God's Glory

UNVEILED

One Woman's Experience
with the Glory of God

Generational Curses Unveiled

Copyright © 2012 by Rebecca L. King

ISBN 978-0-9850810-0-3

Printed in USA by King Publications

<u>Dedication</u>

To my great friend Daph, you left way too early.

Daphne Lee

1965-1995

Memories never fade away.

Table of Contents

Acknowledgments

First of all, I want to thank my Heavenly Father for allowing the truth of His presence to saturate me and make me whole, Jesus for His gift that redeemed my soul and the Holy Spirit for guiding me to my eternal goal.

To the best parents a daughter could ever have. You guys are great! Your faith in raising me for Him has overwhelmed my being. Thanks for the opportunities that you both gave me as you gave yourselves to Him. You're awesome parents and greatly loved. To Scotty, my brother, you are my John the Baptist. You have always prepared the way for your little sister to come forth. My love and appreciation towards you are as red stripes on a candy cane. My precious sister Lori, I have always admired your courageous acts of compassion to always make a prosperous way for others. You are a virtuous woman and I love you so. To my one and only brother-in-law, peace and much love, man. To my anointed nephews, always walk in the truth of God's love and you will forever reap His joy. To my niece Mattie, may your personality of God's presence forever reign. I love you guys.

To my little Eli, you were not born from my womb but formed in my heart. I loved you before I knew you and you have stolen my eyes for all of eternity. To Miranda, my firstborn (leader) of many, you are so beautiful to your mom. Anna, my prophetess, may the words of our God always echo in the voice of your songs. To all of my children that survived "Ms. Becky's boot camp," to God be all the glory. Unconditional love can't touch the way that I feel for all of my children.

To my friend Gail, thanks for all the countless hours of prayer and intercession, all those days and nights of revelation upon revelation. Thanks for always taking me back to what the word promises me as a child of God. Your presence and persistence project the very possession of Jesus Christ's power. I will always be grateful for the way that you followed me around taking notes to orchestrate, articulate and anticipate this project. May the Lord return unto you and your family a thousand fold royal inheritance. I love you friend.

To my photographer Mary, thanks for capturing the glory of God. You're a true picture of His love.

To Evelyn Fox for making things happen!

To Hanna, the greatest friend I ever had.

Mark, thanks for always coming to my rescue, you are an expression of God's provision, and I cherish and honor you.

To the Wednesday Bible Study Group, thanks for having ears to hear.

Shout out to TEAM GLORY. Thanks for loving me guys! Teddy, Ann S., Elizabeth H. and Gail P. for all that you proofed. For all others that helped in any way make this project prosper. May the Lord Bless you and keep you in His arms forever.

Thanks to my friend Jo Ann Josey for introducing me to the World Wide Web.

Foreword

On a particular day, a Sunday, on Valentine's Day, the Heavenly Father demonstrated His love for His daughter, Rebecca Lynn King by giving her a vision that has enabled her to realize destiny.

Much of this material will be new for readers and that is the true purpose of revelation. Revelation is the act of revealing or communicating divine truth–something that is revealed by God to humanity, in this case revealed to Rebecca. Because of this encounter, the vision has become a life message.

Soon after Rebecca had this encounter, she came to me explaining what had transpired. Just minutes into the conversation, I knew what she had experienced was real and declared, "Lay your hands on me. Please give me an impartation of what you have received."

Without hesitation this mighty woman of God began to pray and impart the blessing of the Lord into my life, so much so, that my life has forever been changed in the Glory of God. Because of her vision and its "Divine Intervention," I have witnessed in Rebecca and those she ministers to, breakthrough into new realms simply by sharing the vision of what had been hidden concerning the mysteries of God!

"The Well of God's Glory Unveiled" will give the reader many practical applications that will lead to breaking generational bondages, healing of emotional trauma, as well as teaching how to live in His Glory. The revelation given concerning "The Glory" in itself will put to rout every demonic attack with its application.

I challenge every reader to teach the principles found on the following pages to friends and family members, and thus set the captives free.

I also declare blessings for Rebecca and this book. May readers be found all over the world. May restoration be found in dysfunctional families, healing and deliverance for the sick and bound. And I declare this book and its life lessons will get into the hands of the right people, and that they in their environment and jurisdiction will indeed destroy the works of the devil.

Lemuel David Miller, Apostle
Jacksonville, Georgia
China Hill International Ministries

Endorsement

Rebecca King is a Kingdom General sent for not just the churches, cities, territories and regions, but for Global reformation and transformation. God (Commander and Chief), has given her marching orders in the earth realm to fulfill Habakkuk 2:14 which states, *"For the earth shall be filled with the knowledge of the Glory of the Lord as the waters cover the sea"*. Rebecca has been chosen as a 21st century Esther and has been sent to the Kingdom for such a time as this. She has connected the "Chronos" – extension continuation with the "Kairos" – Proper strategic time to enter into the "Pleroo"- fullness of time in releasing this book. Galatians 4:4 states, *"but when the fullness of time came, God sent forth His Son, born of a Woman"*. John 15:16 states, *"Ye have not chosen me but I have chosen you and ordained you that you should go and bring forth fruit and that your fruit should remain"*.

The seed of God the Father released into Rebecca's spiritual womb has produced fruit that will usher many souls into deliverance, healing, and restoration. Rebecca King truly carries an Issachar Anointing (Duet. 27:12), and she understands the timing and Divine Government of God to release blessings on the People of God. Allow this book to Minister to the chambers of your heart and permeate the windows of your soul, so you can be supernaturally Christ-centered Revolutionized.

Dr. Nancy Tillman-Franklin CEO & Founder
Dr. Nancy Tillman-Franklin Foundation Ministries, Inc.
Hinesville, Georgia

Endorsement

"How's that working for you?", this is a question that we often hear Rebecca ask. It is a question that we have often addressed in our own lives when we keep doing things the way we have been taught, but get no results. If you are one of those people then this book is for you.

If you are a person that feels you have hit a stump in the road that you cannot get past, no matter how hard you try, then this book is for you. It will show you why the stump is in the road, but greater than that how to uproot the stump and clear the way to move on.

As you walk with Rebecca through her experiences take hold of the "revelation" that God has given her as to "why" things are the way they have become and learn how to change your circumstances and walk in the freedom that God designed for each of our lives. It really has not been "working for us". It is time for us to make a change.

Within the pages of this book you will learn how to make those changes and move into your freedom. It is time to move to "revelation" through relationship and not religion. Religion has altered our perspective of God and His ability and His greatness, but revelation will move you to a higher plane of relationship and deeper revelation of not only God but His word. It is that revelation that you will find written in the pages of this book.

I have been with Rebecca for about a year now but our history goes back over 15 years. I have watched as hundreds of people have been totally set free of the things in their lives that have held them in chains, bringing not only deliverance but physical healing. I watch week after week as people who have been caterpillars for so many years they do not even remember when life was any different, become the most beautiful butterflies in the Kingdom of God. They have now gotten over "themselves" and the distractions that their circumstances have placed them into, and are now fully focused on God and His plans and purposes for their lives. We cannot go forward holding on to the past.

As Rebecca moved into the realm of the "Glory of God" (the manifestation of the presence of the Holy Spirit) she found everything was different, as she embraced that difference she found her healing and we pray that as you read you will find yours.

Jo Ann Josey
Apostle, Pastor and Friend.
Warehouse Ministries International
Macon, Ga.

Introduction

For many years, I felt as if I had been entrapped by my own emotions, until I realized that the plans of the enemy were a plot to destroy me and my destiny. I had all of these past pains (like vines) entangled within the timeless hidden chambers of my heart that prevented me from becoming who God had created me to be. When I looked into the mirror, I didn't know who I saw. I was a stranger to myself! I hesitantly had thoughts of trying to learn myself, but feared rejecting my own being.

How did I get to this place? When did my life turn into my struggle? What does my purpose have to do with God's plan? These were just a few questions that soared within my mind, finding nowhere to settle. My life on a daily schedule was full, but always felt empty. It seems like the older I became the more distant I was from the reality of His eternal presence. My mind was exhausted by the many frustrations that bombarded my intellect, but I still longed to be free. Free from what? **Free from me!**

God took me on an adventure to find the hidden treasure of my heritage. He uncovered the well of revelation that I drank from that healed the intimate wounds of my soul. He allowed me to recapture the childlike faith that I enjoyed as a kid playing on my family's farm.

Life should always be an adventure. He revealed to me through this process that the fountain of youth is the answer to the age old questions of renewal. I found the living waters from a well that had been hidden by curses that the enemy had concealed to cancel the thirst that had been quenched by apparent adversities.

As I embarked upon this journey to find wholeness, I realized the importance of being real to myself as well as others. I was frightened to be myself because I was afraid that I would fail. It was easy to act genuine to others, but I finally succumbed to the exhaustion of such a heavy deception. If I was ever going to be all that He created me to be, it was here and it was now.

It seemed as if my life as a Christian had lost its color and flavor, lifeless to its existence. Waiting on things that may never arrive; stuck. Suddenly, things turned as I allowed the Holy Spirit to deliver me into my destiny. I was the one holding up this process of wholeness. I had to acknowledge my areas of delusions and become more aware of my need for Him to cut me loose from every vine of time that had held me captive.

I had become the statue on the cover of this piece of art that God gave me to sculpt, full of cracks from the past. Here, the Holy One was present to take me away from my afflictions and melt me with His love and passion. My circumstances had become cementitious, which complimented the condition of my heart.

With every emotionless effort that I had to offer, I decided to lean on Him. Hardened by my past pains of heaviness, I decided to give Him permission to fill me with His power. As He saturated me with His love, the hardness of my heart began to melt like the wax that runs down a candle stick from the heat of its flame. This was the point that I was healed and then was able to love myself and others.

Allow me to take you intimately through the pages of this book and share with you the incentives that got me through some of the most difficult days of my life. This book is a journal of events and issues that kept me outside of God's promises, until His glory delivered me into my destiny. My prayer is that as you search the depths of your heart through the chapters of this lifelike presentation of my purpose, that you too will find answers to your agonies alongside of triumphs for your victories. May you uncover and discover the hidden well of your heart and receive the living waters of life. As I write this, it has now been seven hundred and thirty days that I have been free from me.

Rebecca L. King

CHAPTER 1

FOR THE WELL IS DEEP

Butterflies filled my stomach as the very thought of catching my father looking away once again entered my mind. If I can just get close enough to take one glance at this underworld, how I knew that it would bring my eight-year old soul satisfaction! My opportunities would arise and then fall, as the sound of the tractor would come near and then fade away, as the numerous ruts that occupied each field demanded my father's attention. Time was crucial. The sunlight dimmed as it slowly crept behind the outline of "them 'ole Georgia pines." I knew if I was going to visit this forbidden hole of atrocity, it must be here, and it must be now. As my anticipation excelled, I began to move forward to this place that I would never return from. Reality slipped away, and my determination overstepped all previous boundaries. I and this place were about to become one.

The sound of the snapping twigs under my feet reminded me of crossing a swing bridge before its final collapse. Before time became my enemy, I must spring forth for this was my last chance. My appetite for adventure prevailed over every emotion that tried to detour my effectiveness. I longed to smell, feel, taste, hear, and see what had been mysterious for countless generations in the past. My senses were in full participation, and my body was impressed by the rhythm of my heartbeat, as we drew nigh to the historical happening. Suddenly, my attentiveness changed directions, as my father approached my area of delusion.

"Becky Lynn, I told you to stay away from this place! Now go get in the truck. It's time to go home."

The ride home was longer than ever this particular evening, simply because of the awkward silence that escorted us safely home. My father is a man of very few words, and in this situation "few" wasn't even found in his vocabulary. My father had an unusual way of expressing himself, so his silence was my only form of communication. My respect for him held my attention and my little mouth from asking,

"Why couldn't I just go look one time Daddy?"

My innocence left me feeling as if I deserved to be clued in on such an important matter. Nevertheless, Dad never addressed the issue and common knowledge led me to bed early that night with unanswered questions.

This experience is still fresh in my mind as I reminisce about the family farm that my father was raised on, and the **"forbidden hole of atrocity"** called the farm well. He instructed me as a child never to get close to it because it was old, and I might fall in and drown. This lack of explanation caused a life time of curiosity. I'm not sure if his fearful instructions were passed down from one generation to another or the lack of my grandfather's parental protection drove my father's concern, but it was definitely my father's focus.

Recently, I had a vision (a vision is something that the Lord shows you in absence of current reality) of an old well, and the Lord directed me to go over and look down into the well. Assuming that this was the well (on my dad and grandfather's farm) that I had played around as a child, I was intrigued as the Lord unveiled this lifelong quest to me. I began to explain to the Lord that my natural father told me not to get around the well, and that I was afraid to get near it. The lack of his explanation was evidence of false intimacy that formed my insecurities. True intimacy offers in-depth explanation.

The Lord reassured me that it would be all right, and that my natural father instructed me out of his own fears. My father in the natural caused this fear within me that was formed out of a lack of communication, so therefore, My Heavenly Father wanted to heal this area with His explanation, which is revelation. Open access to this arena aroused a fear giant inside of me to become very uncomfortable, as it succumbed to this majestic atmosphere.

This uncharted terrain of unfamiliarity was about to be explored by my purposeful intentions of regaining generational territory. What I had feared my whole life was about to be revealed. As I approached the well in the vision, the Lord guided me to—*"Trust in the Lord with all thine heart; and lean not unto thine own understanding. In all thy ways acknowledge Him, and He shall direct thy paths (Proverbs 3:5-6 KJV)."* His word gave me strength in the vision to lean over the old well and look down into the depths of all impossibilities.

I finally had the opportunity of explanation that captivated my curiosity. As I looked over the side and down into the well, the Lord asked me, *"What do you see?"* I said, *"Lord, for the well is deep."* He said, *"Look harder and tell me what you see."* Amazingly, I saw my reflection in the water at the bottom of the well. Several weeks after this vision, I shared what God had revealed to me with my church, never imagining that what was about to take place would be life changing for me and many others.

My Opportunity For A New Heart

This Valentine's Day was like all others, except for the fact that it was on Sunday this particular year. I went to church early to make sure everything was ready for the service, and I felt the Lord drawing me. He wanted me to spend the day with Him (my first love). For the past few months, He had been ministering to me that He desired me to go back to where I first believed and where I first fell in love with Him. It was almost as if it was like that day at the well when I was a little girl again. I actually felt His power and love drawing me, as I did as a child at the **"forbidden hole of atrocity."** It was as if my childhood adventure was welling up inside of me again to fulfill and finalize its mission.

I called my fiancee and asked him if it would be alright with him for me to take the day off and spend time with the Lord. He agreed that it was a wonderful idea and to take as long as I needed. I made a few more phone calls and took care of all my Sunday responsibilities and was able to be released to share my day with the Lord. It's amazing how many phone calls I had to make to handle my schedule just to spend a day with the Lord. We need to be real careful not to be too busy for God. Little did I know that God was about to take me step-by-step through a six hour open vision (an open vision is something that the Lord has revealed to you in the spirit and then it comes to pass in the natural) that He had just shown me weeks before.

I love to ride motorcycles, so I jumped on one of my bikes and began riding on the old dirt roads around my family's farm. God led me to my great-grandfather's farm just several miles away. I wasn't familiar with this farm because my great-grandfather died before I was born and my great-grandmother died when I was a toddler. I had heard my father speak of the ol' home place, but I never knew much more than it's location. I never even considered that this was the place that I would be introduced to what God had planned for me that would rearrange my whole being. Not only was I going back to re-visit my childhood fears, God was leading me to go a generation deeper.

I felt peace after I got off my bike and began wandering around. The Lord led me to the one hundred year old mule stall barn that my great-grandparent's buggy was still parked under. The Lord directed me to get up on the buggy and sit there. As I obeyed the still small voice of the Lord, I thought it a bit strange to be sitting there all alone in a buggy that my ancestors had ridden in over a half a century ago. The Lord began to illustrate to me my great-grandmother's fears and anxieties and assured me that the curse was about to be broken (Ex. 34:7). Even though I didn't really know my great-grandmother, it was if I could feel her pain. I experienced emotions of a full life of prosperity, but an empty heart. I wanted to get down as quick as I got up there to get away from this feeling. I actually saw an image of her face (even though I don't remember her), only to see a photo later that confirmed her features. As I began to dismount this ancient artifact, I thought that it was a bit humorous that I had actually been sitting backwards on the buggy, which explains a major curse that I was under. Has it ever seemed as if you take two steps forward and five backwards? This may be a curse!

I continued my journey from there out into an orchard and sat beneath an old pecan tree, as the Lord continued to roll back the heavenlies in magnificent revelation. I looked beside me and noticed a rather large hole beside my foot and fear began to knock on my chest cavity, along with the guest of adrenaline. Anyone that lives in South Georgia knows that snakes can be found in holes, so my instinct impressed me to reconsider my assigned position. Unfortunately, I was unable to obtain my awareness toward what God was speaking because of the continuous thoughts of how close I was to danger. Finally, I got up and continued on through the orchard and sat at a different location only to discover yet another distinct reptilian residence.

The Lord ministered to me about His Word in Isaiah 11:8 (KJV) *"And the sucking child shall play on the hole of the asp, and the weaned child shall put his hand on the cockatrice' den."* The devil is always around stirring up trouble and causing unnecessary fears that eventually turn into drastic torments, even if you change churches! The Lord tells us in the Word that, *"He would never leave us nor forsake us, and lo I am with you always" (Heb. 13:5, Matt. 28:20)*. This means no matter where the enemy tries to hide, Jesus is with us! ***Praise the Lamb of God.***

You can change churches but God wants to change you.

At this point, it was obvious to me that the enemy apparently had plans to attempt interception, but eternal intercession had already been activated (Rom. 8:34).

I guess that this would be a good place to explain to you the state of mind in which I was in. At this time in my life, I had accomplished a lot as a business owner and minister of the gospel. I had also established a children's home and actually lived there with them. My ministry was also successful and an incredible outreach in our community. I was a very independent, but busy woman. I somehow knew that there was more to life than the success that I had already achieved, but couldn't quite put my finger on why I wasn't more complete than I was. Success doesn't complete you, only the peace of God can accomplish this.

I knew that there was more to life, but didn't know how to get to it. I'm not talking about more success; I'm talking about more joy and peace. I guess you can say that I was *burned out!* On the outside it looked as if I had it all together, but on the inside I was dying daily. By the way, I was a minister of the gospel, so I couldn't dare express my distress!!! If you are in the ministry and try to hide your humanism, you might want to consider repenting for pride. My pride would not let me be real with others about my weaknesses. I was desperate and hopeless and continued to place a smile on my misery of presentation. I actually told God on this Valentine's morning, "either heal me or kill me." Little did I know that all He needed was my permission, and His plans were about to unfold.

God will use our desperation as a tool of separation from our own will.

There was a huge limb that had fallen on the ground and was still attached to the tree; it had partial life (kind of like me). Even though it was broken, it was still somewhat attached, which brought forth evidence of hindered growth. We as Christians sometimes are hindered by our brokenness, which prevents us from maturing in Christ. I heard the enemy's voice encouraging me to go back to the barn, find a rope, tie it to the broken limb, jump from it, and hang myself. The enemy tried to convince me that I was like that limb and that I would always be broken. *"Cursed is anyone who hangeth upon a tree"* (Gal. 3:13). As the enemy encouraged me, he forgot to tell me that the curse was also about to be broken because Jesus Christ became the curse so that we could be free from all curses. The enemy thought that if he could provoke me to the point of taking my own life that the chances of the curses being broken would be null and void. I sat there and battled suicidal thoughts...

Excuse me---this is a good time for me to introduce you to what I call a **book break**. Take 5 minutes, put the book down and ask yourself a valuable question...

Is this book for me?

You need to know that if you have ever battled suicidal thoughts, you are not alone. There is a battle according to Ephesians 6 that is going on right now. The devil desires to "steal, kill, and destroy" (John 10:10), and any way that he can accomplish our demise, he will go for it. Many people take their own lives in desperation of their situations. The enemy's job is to de-spiritualize you in a delusive manner, so that you take on the guilt of not being able to handle circumstances that are out of your control. In all actuality, it never has been about your control, because God is in control.

I actually experienced (in the spirit) my own funeral service which lasted well over an hour. I heard what different ones said as they walked past the casket. One particular man that just happens to be my insurance salesman said, "If Becky couldn't make it, then I sure can't." I saw my family walk hand-in-hand and arm-in-arm. It broke my heart to see the unnecessary pain they were experiencing. My precious father is usually the strong one, but he had to be held up by my mother and helped to his seat. Satan forgets to tell us how bad our families suffer when one of God's children is talked into taking their own life. If you have battled

21

these thoughts, just know that the devil wants you stopped because of your purpose in life. Most of the people that commit suicide feel as if no one loves them or no one cares. The most packed funeral services are the ones that have committed suicide and all the people who come are the ones that the person thought that didn't care. *Keep on striving, don't give up, and you will make it, my friend.*

In this same time frame (in the natural) my church family, not knowing where I was or what I was dealing with, felt led to stop the service, and a man stood up and said, *"That he felt that the people should stretch their hands towards the southwest area,* (exactly where I was located) *and pray for their pastor."* God works in mysterious ways, doesn't He? Suddenly, I felt as if I had been lifted up out of such a horrific struggle. We need to be real sensitive to the Spirit of God when He lays someone on our heart and pray for them right then (Eccl.3:1).

I continued on to the next area that I felt the Lord was leading me. As He led me to the edge of a wooded area, I told the Lord, *"I don't want to go into this place."* He said, *"Will you trust Me?"* I said, *"Yes, God, but I don't want to go in there."* He said again, *"Trust me with your whole heart and lean not unto your own understanding, I will make a way for you, and you will be fine."* It's easy to say that we trust God, in all actuality if our hearts aren't whole, then our trust is broken as well.

The places that we dread the most will be our greatest places of deliverance.

There was only one problem here, my heart was in a hot mess and at this time, that was all that I understood. When our hearts are in such a turmoil, it's hard to understand the things concerning our lives and the life that He has made available for us. I told God that I needed Him to fix my heart and He told me that He couldn't!!! I was shocked at His response. I said, *"God, I thought that you could do anything."* He said, *"I can only do what you allow me to. You won't let me fix your broken heart because you constantly hold on to what has been done to you from the past."* This was a fresh revelation to me because I had actually blamed Him unconsciously for my lack of healing. He quickly responded, *"I don't want to heal your old heart, I want to give you a brand new heart. A heart of wisdom and understanding."* It was then that He gave me this scripture to lean on:

> So teach us to number our days, that we may get us a heart of wisdom.
>
> Psalm 90:12, AMP

Gird Up And Go Into An Open Door

Availability for a new heart will open doors in the spirit realm, but we must have courage to walk on in. Just as Caleb and Joshua knew that they were well able to go into the promise land (Num.13:30), we too must know that we are well able to go into an open door to receive a new heart.

Emotionally exhausted, I obeyed God's request to go further into the woods, only to find inside the wood line an old deep well overtaken by years of vine growth. The way my hands were shaking, you would have thought that the Lord asked me to pull a tooth from a Tyrannosaurus Rex. Fear will always try to keep you from finding ancient answers. We need to realize that as God's children, Satan tries to keep us from finding our answers in life. Revelation and truth are always just steps away, but we must first walk through dread and fear to get to them. In other words,

God's revelation is just on the other side of your dread.

I didn't want to go into this secluded section simply because of my fears, but my faith urged me into this adventure. Faith will always be with us as we step out, and overcome the very things from which our fears have hindered us. ***Hallelujah!*** Faith always produces peace and joy to accompany us on our loneliest journeys. I noticed that a tree (of

23

all things) was growing out of the top of the well. This was a little strange to me, but how much did I really know about wells anyway?

At this point everything was **rare** and **bizarre!**

God has a well of revelation that He desires us to draw nigh to and look down into for His truth. I walked over to the well and got as close as I could without getting too tangled up in all the weeds and vines of time. The ol' home place of my great-grandparents was built in the early 1900's, so I figured that this well was at least 100 years old, and by the look of it, maybe even older. Leaning beside the well was a single board that looked as if it had been used at one time as a part of a frame for a pulley device for a water bucket. The Lord directed me to begin breaking the vines to get closer to the well. I told God that there were too many vines to be broken, and I had nothing with which to cut them. He instructed me that the vines **represented curses** that were on my family from generations ago, and if I would break the vines, I would receive everything back that my ancestors had lost to the enemy.

> Keeping mercy and loving-kindness for thousands, forgiving iniquity and transgression and sin, but Who will by no means clear the guilty, visiting the iniquity of the fathers upon the children and the children's children, to the third and forth generation.
>
> Exodus 34:7, AMP

Even though my ancestors had plenty and never lost their earthly possessions to poverty, they lost their joy and peace and longevity of life. If we don't have joy and peace, how can we enjoy earthly possessions (in-joy)? The Lord encouraged me that He was so big that He would go back generations and bring forth the blessings of which my ancestors didn't take possession of and give them to me because of my obedience. He even told me that my obedience had brought forth enough power to set others free when they would hear this testimony. If I would **get over myself** and share this with others, then He would set them free.

24

IF you will listen diligently to the voice of the Lord your God,
being watchful to do all His commandments which I command
you this day, the Lord your God will set you high above all the
nations of the earth. And all these blessings shall come upon
you and overtake you if you heed the voice of the Lord your
God.

Deuteronomy 28:1-2, AMP

And I will restore *or* replace for you the years that the locust
has eaten-the hopping locust, the stripping locust, and the
crawling locust, My great army which I sent among you.

Joel 2:25, AMP

With a vengeance, I went into the maze of years of growth, breaking vine after vine (Matt.11:12), and what looked impossible was being made possible (Matt. 19:26). The more impossible things seem in the natural is mere confirmation that spiritual possibilities are available. The Lord instructed me that I didn't need a cutting instrument to get through the tough vines, that I could use His Word. The Bible says that it is *"sharper than any two-edged sword, cutting between soul and spirit, between joint and marrow. It exposes our innermost thoughts and desires. Nothing in all creation is hidden from God. Everything is naked and exposed before His eyes and He is the One to whom we are accountable" (Heb. 4:12-13 NKJ)*. God's Word is revelation, and revelation brings forth exposure.

As I took hold of them, I spoke the Word of God and they began to crack and separate, one by one. I began to gain ground that once was overgrown with my enemy's victory. Unaware of time, I didn't let up until I was standing right in front of what I thought to be my destiny. Don't give up; your destiny is right around the corner from your misunderstandings. Misunderstandings stem from fear because we normally fear what we don't know. If you actually knew how close you were to your destiny, you would break on through. Come on in friend, you are almost there!

We see a clear analogy of our lives in II Kings 7 when the lepers were faced with their situation of dying outside of their destiny. Their question was to each other, **"Why do we sit here until we die?"** We are all eventually going to die, so we might as well die going in. They had to *get over themselves* before they went into their destiny. Hopefully, you'll be interested enough to read II Kings 7 and find out the rest of their victory story. We need more victory stories instead of victim stories!!! The Word of God says, *"That we overcome the enemy by the blood of Jesus and the word of our testimonies" (Rev. 12:11).*

I felt the Lord tugging at my heart once again.....*To lean not unto thine own understanding, lean on My truth*, so I jumped at the opportunity to lean over the side of this ancient artifact. At this point, this seemed more like a segment in an Indiana Jones movie, someone looking for a lost treasure. As I looked over into the depths of this man-made hole, I expected to find the lost treasure of my heritage, and all I saw was my boring reflection once again in the water at the bottom of the well. I never considered that I was,

THE LOST TREASURE!

I threw my head back and hollered up to the heavenlies, *"What is this God? What do you want from me? Are you trying to kill me?"* I felt a small response of *"Yes"* from His presence. Remember, I told the Lord in my desperate state, *"Lord, heal me or kill me."* My human emotions at this time, were very aggravated. I said, *"Yes? Yes? What God? Yes, what?"* Again, I felt His warm presence saying, *"Yes, I want your old nature to die."*

I had been studying for years and asking God to explain to me why the Israelites did not enter into the Promise Land. At this particular time, I found my answer. The Israelites couldn't...

"Get over themselves."

Get over themselves, *"God, What does this mean, God?"* He replied, *"They never saw themselves as the lost treasure! They had been in bondage their whole lives and could not see themselves as My chosen nation. They were so accustomed to slavery, that they could not get use to the truth of their freedom. Just like you! You can't walk in My Promise Land Plan, and take your own route as well. You either have to make a sacrifice and trust Me for direction or lean on your own understanding only to wander around your whole life. You have to be willing to **GET OVER YOURSELF** for My will to be done in your life. This journey that you have been on has been a repetitious one that has left you empty from your own adventures that were adapted from your forefathers. I made you in My own image to contain My glory but because of the fall of mankind, I had to make you out of an earthly substance called dust as a secondary means of submission. I desire My people to choose me over their brokenness. True submission takes trust. In My image you are whole, but in your earthen image you have become broken by all the pains from your past. Anything that is created from dust/dirt is breakable. In order to overcome your brokenness you must submit to me with your whole heart and break through your brokenness. To do this you must be willing to trust Me and trade in the old man for the new man. Your new man can and will contain My glory. As you lean on Me I will explain to you about My glory and you will begin to acknowledge My glory. You do not know My glory because you have leaned on your own understanding that was formed out of the broken man. My glory brings My wisdom. I desire to fill you with the knowledge of My glory as the waters cover the seas. As long as you allow your brokenness to be a part of you, you will not be able to contain My glory. My glory must have a place to reside within My people. My people wonder why My promises have not yet come to pass in their lives, and it's only because they say that they are on my path, but yet continue to take their own ways. This way seems like the right way, but the end therefore is deadly. I desire to bless My people, but this can only take place after My people **get over themselves**. I not only want you to take My way, but also* *consider your ways that have led you into captivity. I did not call you to dwell in the desert. I desire for you to dwell in My promises. When you dwell in My promises, then you will be able to help My other children possess My promises. You have been stuck for years wandering around the wilderness like your forefathers, but now as you **get over yourself**-- you can come into My Heavenly Promise of beholding My glory!"*

I responded, *"Lord, I want to **get over myself**, but I don't know how. I desire Your will to come forth in my life and fulfill all of Your promises of Yea and Amen. Will you help me to understand and take a stand for Your glory? Will You teach me why I have come up empty so many times in my life and to help others find this new place as well? Will you explain to me what Your glory is? Will you show me how to trade in my old understanding for Your wisdom and teach me how to have a whole heart full of Your glory? Lord, show me Your glory! I want to,*

"GET OVER MYSELF"

The peace of God came over me as I agreed with everything that He said concerning my life and that I wanted to **get over myself** more than anything that I had ever wanted before. I had no idea how to accomplish what He had shown me and needed Him to explain every detail of His master plan. At this point I realized that there was a lot that I thought I knew, but His presence proved that even my righteousness was as filthy rags. I knew in order to know Him, I must embrace this place of my emptiness to find His promises. His presence desired to quench my thirst, but it was up to me to drink from this cup.

Will you travel with me on this journey to find the hidden treasure of who we really are?

Here we go, we want to
GET OVER OURSELVES!!!

May I lead you in a prayer before we go any further?

Dear Gracious Heavenly Father,

I thank You for this opportunity to allow us to go into the depths of our souls and search out the deepest parts of our beings. We thank You, Lord, that You have met us at the well of our lives to give us a drink of revelation, concerning the hidden mysteries that have held us in bondage for generations. We thank you that you have not left us the way we are. You love us so much that you want us to be free from any and all curses that would keep us from entering into Your promises. We thank you that the veil of ignorance has been lifted off of us to see Your truth. We repent of any way that we have allowed our fears to ostracize us from all truths, which would prevent or frustrate our deliverance. We ask that You give us spiritual ears to hear and spiritual eyes to see what Your Spirit is teaching us in this hour. May our hearts be mended and our minds be still as Your wind blows forth fresh fire of revelation. In Jesus' Name.

NOTES

NOTES

CHAPTER 2

BE VICTORIOUS INSTEAD OF A VICTIM

The first thing that God began to show me was that I had enough self-pity to keep myself in bondage for the rest of my life. In order to **get over myself**, I was going to have to reposition myself. I had to get over my emotions, instead of being under them. God made us to have control over our emotions, but if we are broken, they usually have control over us. Not only did I have self pity, but I also felt sorry for others as well. I found myself giving to other people out of my brokenness. We must first realize our own brokenness before God can make us whole. This was the next step into my adventure. I was so broke that I was paying everyone else's bills. I actually felt like that I was accomplishing a lot because it made me feel somewhat worthy. I didn't even realize that I had been a victim to my own brokenness. As long as we keep a victim mentality, we will never become victorious.

Self-Pity is the foundation of victimization. Sympathy is a dressed up word for pity. Jesus had compassion for the people, not sympathy. You may say, *"Well, you don't know what I have been through."* Neither do you know what I have been through, but we are not the focus here, nor is anyone trying to win the a prize for the most brokenness. Our focus should be on Him, the King of Kings, and the Lord of Lords, who is more than willing and able to separate us from our afflictions. In order for victory to take its place, there must be a shift in the way that we think about ourselves, including the thought about the wrong that has been done to us. If you constantly remind yourself of how wrong you have been done, then you will never have the opportunity to be free.

When Jesus was on the cross, He said, *"Forgive them Father, for they know not what they do" (Luke 23:34)*. Jesus is still the example of forgiveness, and if we follow Him, we also have to follow His examples. We must forgive **whoever** for **whatever** in order to find healing for ourselves. If we feel sorry for ourselves, then we will neglect forgiveness. When forgiveness is activated in our lives, then there is a paradigm shift that takes place and suddenly you see yourself no longer as the victim, but victorious. The Word of God in Ephesians 6 speaks of "girding up your loins with truth in order to stand in times of trials." We must gird up if we are going to get over ourselves.

We Must Get Over Our Emotions In Order To Stand

Usually by the time we begin seeking the 6th chapter of Ephesians, it's only because we have already been saturated with the schemes of the evil one. We try to squirm our way out with the self-pity of, "I've done everything I can do; all I can do now is stand." It's the light that we need in the darkest hours. I don't want to just be able to stand; I want to be able to conquer. Romans 13:12 AMP says, *"The night is far gone and the day is almost here. Let us then drop (fling away) the works and deeds of darkness and put on the [full] armor of light."* **Glory to God!** If the Glory Light of God goes before us, He will make a way where there seems to be no way (like a floodlight invading darkness). His Glory Light will illuminate our way for us, and every demon has to flee when the Glory of God is present.

*Lord, we just stop right now and call forth Your Glory upon our hopeless situations, lost loved ones, and ourselves, for the way we hide from the darkness that is within us as if it will one day go away. Teach us how to gird up and stand strong to **get over ourselves** for Your glory. We call forth the light of Your Glory to withdraw every ounce of darkness that is within us that we may be made whole, In Jesus' Name.*

We don't want to just stand, we want to progress and take possession of the land!

I told God, *"I want to go in! I want to **get over myself** Lord, now."* Our brokenness is what keeps us from going into places of wholeness. He instructed me to grab the old rugged board that used to be part of the pulley device and place it over the top of the well, so I did. The board represented the glory of God's provision making a way to extend me to a place that He could take me over myself. Jesus was crucified on an old rugged board (cross) where God extended Him from His natural place into His supernatural place. We need to get to the place of despair that no matter what God asks us to do, we have a deep desire to accomplish the task. God will take you to a place of getting over yourself if you are willing to go. Despair is your friend, because it births a desire within you to choose Him. We must discern the things in our lives that continue to bring destruction and become more aware of these areas, in order for despair to work for us, instead of against us. Despair has the power to bring forth depression if not discerned correctly; but when discerned, despair also has the power to separate you from destruction.

The word *'extend'* in Webster's dictionary means "to make available." If we would make ourselves available for being made whole, then we would be made whole. It is not a matter of if He wants to make us whole; it is a matter of if we will make ourselves available for wholeness. Despair that denies Him and partners with darkness births destruction. Be careful to choose Him.

The next instruction from God took me by total surprise. I thought I heard the Lord say, *"Get on top of the board, look down into the well, and tell me what you see."* I said out loud where God could hear me very plainly, *"O.K., God. I'm sure now that you are trying to kill me."* I placed the old weathered board on top of the well and jumped up on top of it. I wouldn't suggest that you try this at home! We need to get to the point that we jump up, and obey the voice of God no matter what the

33

price. Obedience is better than a sacrifice. Delayed obedience is disobedience. The board began to crack and sway, but I was on it!

I said to God, *"Now what?"* He replied, *"Look down."* I looked down into the depths of my new position only to find again my boring reflection in the water at the bottom of the well. I said, *"God, what are you trying to show me?"* The Lord then replied,

"YOU ARE OVER YOURSELF!"

The Lord said, *"Becky, My dear daughter, precious and loved by Me and many, you have feared yourself for many years, only to come to this conclusion, that I have your best interests at heart. If you will just trust Me and lean on Me, I shall direct your paths. I shall be the living water in your life that you will never thirst again. As you rely on Me, I will replace your heart and give you a voice to the nations, a voice of healing and salvation with many signs and wonders. Trust Me that I know best for every area of your life, not only the areas that you think I'm strong enough to handle. For I am the Great I Am, and I want to be to you* **beyond anything, beyond everything** *that you could ever think or imagine. Lean back on Me and trust Me wholly."*

"Lean back," I thought. *"Lord, I've gotten on a rotten board over a fifteen foot hole in the ground that my great-grandfather built generations ago. Is this not enough?* I heard the Lord say, *"But you still have fear. Lean back. Lean on Me. Trust Me."* In the midst of all my frustration, I jolted back only to be caught by the strange tree growing out of the inside wall of the well.

I heard the Lord say, *"Years ago, I encouraged this little tree to grow in this peculiar place to hold you up when you decided to lean on Me."* It was at this point that I realized that God really could hold me up and it was all according to how I would let myself go. We have a hard time letting ourselves go, when we think that we are the ones that have held ourselves up for so long. We have held ourselves up alright!

We Can't Keep Leaning Back On Our Understanding

Our own understanding is established out of our brokenness, therefore it is a lot of times misunderstanding. Misunderstanding will cause one to mistrust. When we are first introduced into this world, we have somewhat of an advantage over MISTRUST, simply because we have been hidden in the womb for a period of time. In the womb, we may take on the different emotional issues of our parents, but basically we rely fully on the mother to nurture us as we grow. Our dependence on her is involuntary. It takes no thought, it just is. Even though we may sense rejection, fear, or abandonment at times, if the mother is experiencing anxieties, we still are in a position that our trust is exposed. True trust exposes all fears!

From the time of our delivery until the present time, we form our own opinions of how we rely on others or deny (reject) others. Or better yet, the word *'deject'* according to Webster's dictionary, describes what we do to others, which is *"to throw down."* When we were separated from our mother's womb into the womb of this world, we continued the process of trusting involuntarily. As we grew through pains and traumas, we became afraid, and fears began to form us instead of faith. Fear, Rejection, and Abandonment find a place to dwell within us and disfigure us to the point that we begin to believe that we don't really have a purpose, much less a place in this life. You do have a purpose, and God does have a place reserved especially designed with you in mind. It is called **DESTINY**! If you will just keep reading and believe that you are about to enter into one of the best places in your life that you have ever been, you are about to see yourself as He really sees you.

GLORY TO GOD.

We have become fragile from our past pains and failures to the point that we find it hard to trust in ourselves and others. We say that we trust God, but in all actuality we are double-minded in this area of delusion. Double-mindedness is a generational curse that you adopted from others.

35

Double-mindedness is looking in the mirror and not being able to see yourself as God sees you, therefore creating a false intimate relationship with yourself. Your spirit man knows your beauty, and your flesh man can't accept it because of your self-bitterness. At this point, you began to acknowledge the deception; but because of the bitterness, you continue to judge yourself and self-doubt kicks in to take control. This is when we realize that we cannot trust ourselves.

Chances are if you have trouble trusting yourself and others on a day-to-day basis, you deserve to be honest with yourself and realize that you probably don't trust God either. *"A man of two minds (hesitating, dubious, irresolute), is unstable, unreliable and uncertain about everything" (James 1:8 AMP).* Have you ever felt unstable in all of your ways? This may contribute to not fully relying and trusting in a God you have never seen before. Let's just take care of this right now with repentance, and see what God has for us in this forth coming chapter.

Dear Heavenly Father,

I come to You in the name of Jesus and repent for being double-minded and unstable in all of my ways. Forgive me Lord, for the way I have justified my doubt and unbelief. I've allowed myself to think that I trusted You, but in all truth, I have not trusted You. Please forgive me for saying and acting like I trusted You when really I was full of fear and was afraid that You would not help me. Lord, I am ready to fully trust You and become victorious. I want to lean on Your truth instead of my understanding, which is usually misunderstanding. I want to get over myself right here and right now for Your glory to come forth in my life. Lord, forgive me for the way that I've blamed You for bad things happening in my life, when the enemy was at fault. I also forgive myself for any way that I have failed in all areas of mistrust. I cancel this debt and all of Satan's tormentors. Holy Spirit, tell me Your truth concerning trust.

Why We Don't TRUST

The Lord began to show me how fragile life had made me. The Webster's dictionary defines *'fragile'* as "easily broken or destroyed." If there is an area of our lives that contains a weak link, then eventually there will be brokenness. We must repent of fear, and allow our faith to mend these places before the enemy causes more damage. When we realize and believe that God is for us and not against us, then we can trust. True intimacy encourages and strengthens us to believe that we can actually free fall into God's arms, and He will catch us!

If you are broken, then you probably don't understand what I mean when I say true intimacy. Understanding true intimacy comes when you experience true love. Past failed relationships and heartfelt pains force us not to trust anyone because we assume that we will always get hurt. Not only does God want to heal us of our past pains, but He also wants us to trust Him truly for the first time. When we are healed, then we can truly enjoy a relationship with others, not having to worry about whether or not they are going to hurt us. If you expect someone to hurt you, then your expectation will find a way for a manifestation.

Expectations bring forth Manifestations

It's true intimacy that God desires with us, and anything less would fall under the category of counterfeit. We have to know the difference between true and false intimacy to be free. We will be talking more about this in a later chapter.

Intimacy is gauged by good and bad, just as other things are judged. Discernment knows the difference between good and evil. Mature discernment is choosing good! Too many times we choose to believe that just because we have been hurt by so many others, God will eventually hurt us as well. Not true! Too many times we also believe our understanding to be the only answer. God gets blamed for a lot of

37

things that occur in our lives when we don't rightly discern and/or understand.

List the things in which you have blamed God and others for:
(Be HONEST)

Now may I lead you through a prayer?

Dear Heavenly Father,

I purpose and choose with my free will to repent for any and all ways that I have blamed you and others for bad things happening in my life. I ask that You will forgive me and I forgive myself. Holy Spirit please come and heal my broken heart and speak your words of truth.

> My people are destroyed for lack of knowledge; because you [the priestly nation] have rejected knowledge, I will also reject you that you shall be no priest to Me; seeing you have forgotten the law of your God, I will also forget your children.
>
> Hosea 4:6, AMP

Before we can *"get over ourselves,"* we must repent and replace our ignorance with knowledge, and stop this process of destruction. We gamble with a handful of fear while bluffing at our opponent with a heart weakened by past games of failure. We then choose to blame God when we lose everything because we didn't lay our faith down on the table. We must take responsibility for our catastrophic lifestyles, and stop accusing God of our downfalls. He is the God of all creation, and *"He is able to meet all of our needs according to His riches in glory"* (Phil. *4:19)*. If things in our lives haven't worked out just right, then we need to ask ourselves a question as to whether we have unconsciously misjudged our discernment about God, and how His allowance of bad happenings has birthed bitterness within our hearts.

In other words, if you think that God allowed these bad things to happen to you, and/or maybe caused them to happen, then there will be a level of what I call "**unconscious accusations**" against God.

Unconscious Accusations are judgments that
we place on God for allowing things to
happen to us and blaming Him for what
the enemy takes from us.

We automatically assume that whatever takes place in our lives is because God allows them to come forth. Again, this is a misunderstanding that brings forth mistrust concerning God and others. These are assumptions that leave us empty; therefore causing us to place blame on God unconsciously, and this eventually causes a level of bitterness to spring up within us, which is the enemy's plan. God is the only one Who can heal us of our past anguishes and present torments, so there must be an exchange of apologies.

God is full of love, forgiveness, and acceptance. He has His side covered. Remember, He is our original, eternal, ultimate covering! If we have a hard time trusting and understanding God, then we will have a hard time forgiving ourselves and others. We must now *"humble ourselves, pray, and seek His face that we may be healed" (II Chr. 7:14)*. If I tell my kids not to play in the road because they may get hurt and then they play in the road and get hurt, did I allow this? No! God doesn't allow things to happen to us just to say, "I told you so." If we have unconscious accusations against God, this prevents Him from healing us because of the judgment that we have against Him. We must first forgive in order to be forgiven!

We Must "HUMBLE" Ourselves

Our brokenness will encourage us to protect ourselves, but this can be a form of pride, if not repented. When you are healed, you don't have to defend yourself. We defend ourselves out of our brokenness. Many times, the very thing that keeps us from apologizing is the fear that it won't be accepted. In some cases, pride will tell you that you have the right to hold on to what you feel. This form of pride and rejection will keep you from receiving your healing. No matter what the situation, pride comes to steal, kill, and destroy.

Humility is one of the first steps that we take to get over ourselves. Whenever we humble ourselves, we make ourselves available for wholeness. I'm here to tell you that God will accept your apology, and this is the next step to your freedom. Forgive, and it shall be forgiven - **100% HEALING!** We must make ourselves available for healing! Repentance always brings restoration. Remember, healings make you whole. This means right NOW. He wants you to believe this and be made whole.

Think about when you discipline your children, and then they walk away to pout. The reason they walk away to pout is because things didn't go their way or maybe someone hurt their feelings. They withdraw themselves because this is a sense of failure, and no one enjoys failure. No matter what the reason, we too are like these little children. We have been pouting long enough. It's time that we repent and get on with the process. We are the one who loses when something (that we allow) comes between us and God, and then we blame Him. Wake up! He doesn't want any division between Himself and His people!

"It grieves Him even for a Saint of His to die," (Ps. 116:15) and it really grieves Him to be blamed for deaths that take place prematurely. Most people think that when people die, it was apparently God's will. This is not so! There is an appointed time of death for each man (Heb. 9:27), but there is also a premature death caused by the enemy that *"steals, kills, and destroys" (Eccl. 7:17)*. Jesus was young when He was crucified. This occurred so the curse of premature death would be broken. Joseph, the father of Jesus, also died prematurely! We need to declare and decree that the days of the righteous are plentiful, and come out of agreement with any deception that would cause the fear of dying young or losing any of our loved ones prematurely to occur. If you have undergone a trauma of losing someone prematurely such as a parent at a young age, be especially careful not to make a vow or agree with the curse that *"if Mama died at 42, then so will I."*

We have to be smarter than the one trying to steal, kill, and destroy. Misunderstanding of God's sovereignty would say that nothing happens without God's allowance. Break the generational curse of premature death and live. I say, "LIVE." Dr. Art Mathias wrote a great prayer manual, *How to Minister Workbook,* that will lead you through trauma prayers to help you get free from these curses.

Have you ever had the thought that someone just honestly died too young? Do you really think that this was your own thinking? The Holy Spirit was trying to minister to you that this person was too young to die.

Ecclesiastes 7:17 (AMP) says, *"[Although all have sinned], be not wicked overmuch or willfully, neither be foolish---why should you die before your time?"* It doesn't please God when teenagers get killed in car accidents or children die of leukemia. He gives life (James 1:17). Satan is the one that "comes to take life."

Another example of brokenness is always trying to blame others for our sufferings. If we blame God for all the bad things that happen, then there will eventually be bitterness, anger, and unforgiveness towards God. Example: If a man kills your child and goes to trial, who do you place judgment on? (the man, of course). If you think that God allowed your son to be killed by the man, then on whom do you place judgment? We must rightly discern this demonic act of premature death and receive the knowledge that replaces all ignorance of any deception that would dilute our faith in a God that protects and provides.

We do live in a world of darkness, according to Ephesians 6. Bad things do happen to good people; but we should have more discernment towards God than we do, because what are the chances of surviving without God's protection and provision? Usually the things that we fear the most come upon us.

I ministered to a widow about the premature death of her husband. He was a pillar in the local church, and a lot of people were really discouraged by the apparent fact that God would take such a man of prominence in a car accident. In all actuality, the wife admitted to me, when I was ministering to her about the truth, God did not take her husband, that the devil stole his life. She just needed someone to confirm what she thought to be true. She also agreed that the plans that her husband made to travel that particular day were hindered in several different occurrences, and she believed that this was God's way of trying to get him to stay home.

Saints, we must be aware of our surroundings. The Holy Spirit will alert us when things in our atmosphere are planning to bring forth harm to us and our loved ones. The Word of God says that the sheep know the Shepherd's voice (John 10:4). Discernment is very important in this hour, and I believe that it is a vital weapon to counterattack the weapons that the enemy has already formed against us (Isaiah 54:17).

Generational Curses of Premature Death can be discerned and disassembled by decreeing and declaring the Word of God!

We will be talking about this later in Chapter Eight "Personalities of Generational Curses."

In order to discern, we must be able to hear clearly. Any form of bitterness hinders the way in which we hear God. Bitterness causes a hardness to form, such as wax that forms in the natural ear drum causing a hindrance to hear clearly. We need to clean out our spiritual ears with the q-tip of repentance and begin to hear once again.

May we pray?

Dear Father,

Please forgive me for not hearing that still small voice that You speak to me in. Forgive me for any misunderstanding or mistrust that I have allowed between the two of us that would hinder me from hearing You. I repent for any and all bitterness and pride that would disable me from receiving Your direction. Lord, I'm sorry for going the wrong way because I so desperately wanted to hear you to the point I said that it was You, and in all actuality, it was my misinterpretation of You. I forgive myself and choose to continue a life of repentance so I can hear You clearly. Help me to come out of any agreements that I may have made in the past that would enable premature death to take place in my life. In Jesus' Name.

In the first 3 chapters of Revelation, the Lord distinctively instructs His saints to have an ear to hear. There have been times when I was traveling down the highway, the Holy Spirit ministered to me to slow down, only to find out later that an accident happened in the same location. When we get over ourselves and are made whole, then we are able to hear.

Discernment Disables Destruction

I had someone ask me one time, "Can the devil kill you?" And my response to this was, "*Yes!*" The Bible says that *"he comes only to steal, KILL, and destroy" (John 10:10)*. It doesn't matter how you look at the word **KILL**, it still means **KILL**. We refer to what Job experienced when God told Satan that he couldn't take Job's life; that isn't always the case (Job 2:6). We can't afford to remain ignorant of the enemy's devices.

My question to this is: What kind of spiritual doors of legal access did Job have open to the enemy? The Bible also talks about if we knew that the thief was coming in the midnight hour, would we not wait up for him (Matt.24:43)? We must have knowledge to develop discernment because the "lack of knowledge will destroy you and your children for generations to come" (Hosea 4:6). The thief can't steal, kill, and destroy if you knock him out first. The weapon that is available for us to use on him is the **"dagger of discernment"** that cuts his authority (head) off. We must reclaim the wisdom that founded our royal inheritance, in order to take back what the devil has stolen from us, our children, and our children's children. When we don't use knowledge to form discernment, we operate under ignorance, and ignorance is the foundation of judgment.

Ignorance is the foundation for judgment.

Ignorance is formed from our misunderstanding. One of the commandments in the Word of God says that, *"You shall not witness falsely against your neighbor" (Ex. 20:16, AMP)*. This commandment is really protecting you more so than your neighbor, simply because when you devise accusations of others, you disable your discernment. It is discernment that God is trying to teach us in this hour to keep us from destruction. We must not only know the truth before it can set us free, but we have to activate and operate in the truth in order for the change to come. If we say that we know the truth but are not changed by it, then it is just head knowledge and not heart knowledge. Head knowledge brings confusion and dissatisfaction, but heart knowledge brings change and satisfaction. We must give God permission to change our mind before our heart can be changed.

I also want to add here that gossip is a form
of murder, and murder slaughters discernment.
Slander is formed out of gossip, and gossip is fueled by accusations,
which are established by judgment.

Be careful not to judge. Judgment disables discernment. The book of Proverbs speaks about how we use our words:

> With his mouth the godless man destroys his neighbor, but through knowledge and superior discernment shall the righteous be delivered.
>
> Proverbs 11:9, AMP

You mean to tell me that the righteous need deliverance? Yes, I am telling you that even the righteous man needs deliverance! Deliverance is what makes him righteous.

> There are those who speak rashly, like the piercing of a sword, but the tongue of the wise brings healing.
> Proverbs 12:18, AMP

> A gentle tongue [with its healing power] is a tree of life, but willful contrariness in it breaks down the spirit.
> Proverbs 15:4, AMP

> Death and life are in the power of the tongue, and they who indulge in it shall eat the fruit of it [for death or life].
> Proverbs 18:21, AMP

45

When we talk negatively about others, this is foreign to the angels because they don't operate in false intimacy. Negative emotions, along with envy and jealousy, will cause you to be murderous. What you think is impossible to accomplish, you judge others for trying to do. Judgment will always find something wrong with someone. False intimacy loves accusations of others. The very thing that we judge, accuse or speak harshly of concerning others will eventually visit us or those that we love. I know a lady that talks terrible about other people's children and wonders why terrible things keep happening to her children. We need to be more merciful instead of murderous! According to Proverbs 14:30 (KJV), *"A sound heart is the life of the flesh: but envy the rottenness of the bones."* Osteoporosis? When we allow ourselves to operate under the influence of envy, it weakens the very marrow of our bones.

The truth behind false intimacy is building a relationship on a foundation of fear, pillars of mistrust, walls of deception, and a covering of insecurities. This façade demonstrates itself by saying that others are less than we are, and that brings comfort to our areas of weakness.

When we neglect our deliverance, we build upon a foundation of deception. This, by the way, introduces us to a curse because the Word of God says, *"Judge not, that ye be not judged. For with what judgment ye judge, ye shall be judged: and with what measure ye mete, it shall be measured to you again" (Matt. 7:1-2, KJV).* Automatic curses are birthed from the lack of knowledge, accusation, and judgment. This will also introduce you to what the medical professionals call autoimmune diseases, which are explained as self-induced afflictions by way of negative emotions that attack our bodies and hold us captive to disease. For more information on spiritual and emotional strongholds to specific diseases, visit www.akwellspring.com and order **In His Own Image** by Dr. Art Mathias.

An *automatic curse* is different than a *generational curse*. An automatic curse comes when we repetitiously rebel against what we know as truth, instead of allowing the truth to set us free. The enemy knows that the truth can set us free, that's why he tries to convince us that there is nothing wrong with us, it's everybody else! We become ensnared by the deception that discourages our wholeness. Automatic curses, if not repented of and broken, can and will turn into a generational curse that we could leave as an inheritance for our children and grandchildren. Let's be real careful to sweep around our own doors. And if our neighbor's door needs sweeping, let's go over and lend a helping hand (you better take a used broom though).

The Word of God says to love our neighbors as we do ourselves (Lev. 19:18, Rom. 13:9-10). The only problem with this is the fact that we really don't love ourselves! We haven't experienced true love (intimacy), so therefore, we automatically operate out of all that we know, which is usually based out of our brokenness.

We can't love our neighbors until we learn how to love ourselves.

The way that we have judged ourselves has left an aftermath of self-bitterness, self-hatred, and unforgiving feelings towards ourselves for the things that we have done in our lives that we knew we shouldn't have done. This is why it is so important to be careful with whom you spend your time. If you yoke up with a co-worker who is notorious for their negative comments of others, you too will find yourself in a negative condition.

Paul says it best when he said, *"Why do I do the things that I don't need to do, and the things that I need to do I don't get done?"* (Rom. 7:15, Author's paraphrase).

We reap what we sow!

47

We must come to a place that we take accountability for our actions and quit blaming others for the things that come to pass in our lives as a result of our own seeds that have been sown in the midnight hour. Remember, you will reap what you have sown. If you sow rejection, you will reap rejection. If you sow fear, you will reap fear. If you sow abandonment, you will reap abandonment. If you sow love then you will reap love. Let's take a look at this scripture:

> Do not be deceived and deluded and misled; God will not allow Himself to be sneered at (scorned, disdained, or mocked by mere pretentions or professions, or by His precepts being set aside.) [He inevitably deludes Himself who attempts to delude God.] For whatever a man sows, that and that only is what he will reap.
>
> Galatians 6:7, AMP

Hurt People, Hurt People.

May I lead you in a prayer?

Dear Father God,

I come to You in the name of Jesus, asking Your forgiveness for the way that I have blamed You for allowing bad things to happen to me and my family. I've been wrongly taught about Your allowance of bad happenings; therefore, I judged You as not loving me. Please forgive me. And I also forgive myself and others for all the ways that I have tried to figure You out, and since I could not, I blamed You and others. Please forgive me for the ways that I have belittled others that I might look strong. I ask that You forgive me for the way that I have believed others and their accusations about others. Dear Jesus, please help me to be able to love myself and others. Teach me how to love and receive love. This process of destruction has to cease. Please help me to see the truth and as I see it, may it set me free.

CHAPTER 3

RENOVATION BRINGS RENEWAL

We have got to start somewhere, why not here? After we realize what brokenness is and the aftermath that it has left behind, it is up to us to be willing to restart and be renewed. We must be willing to begin the renovation process before renewal can bring forth restoration. If it hasn't been working for us, then we need to be willing to rip it out and search for a new way. The word '*renovation*' is defined in the Webster's dictionary as "restoring to life, vigor, or activity: revived, renewed, to make new." The Word of God says that He makes all things **NEW.** You have to be willing to tear out the old to make room, which comes by way of revelation. Revelation takes you into the new. We have to be available for His way over our old ways in order to receive revelation. Revelation is God's explanation. When we don't have the right answers, we seemingly keep trying the wrong ways. I ask myself a personal question about things in my life that kept ending up, upside down:

How's that working for me?

I'll go ahead and ask you the same question, "How is what you have been doing working for you?" If you think that your way is the best way but you aren't getting the fullest results, you might want to trade your way in for His. When we are aggravated by our own failures, it is time to turn from our own ways to His, which is revelation. Hopelessness is evidence of your will!

The Webster's dictionary defines *'revelation'* as an act of revealing or communicating divine truth: something that is revealed by God to humans: an act of revealing to view or making known. There has to be an initial act of faith that causes your free will to excuse itself while renovation takes place, and then you can move on to the renewed things of God. Renovation is often times dreaded because of the mess that it makes. Let me assure you of one thing, you will be more satisfied with the latter than you are with the former. Trust me; better yet, TRUST and LEAN ON HIM!

> And He Who is seated on the throne said, See! I make all things new. Also He said, Record this, for these sayings are faithful (accurate, incorruptible, and trustworthy) and true (genuine).
>
> Revelation 21:5, AMP

We must make a transfer in the Spirit in order for the old things to pass away (**transfers come before transplants**—more about this in Chapter 4). We must be willing to trade the old way (that doesn't work very well) for the new way that will work better. We have settled with the old way because that is what others taught us to do. In all actuality, it didn't work for them and isn't working for us! We must transfer our mindsets from the past painful experiences to the present time of NOW faith according to Hebrews 11.

> NOW FAITH is the assurance (the confirmation, the title deed) of the things [we] hope for, being the proof of things [we] do not see and the conviction of their reality [faith perceiving as real fact what is not revealed to the senses].
>
> Hebrews 11:1, AMP

We can't have **now** faith if we are still living with the scars of yesterday. The ground must be tilled with repentance and made ready to receive the seed in which brings forth the **Harvest of Healing**. We will not be available for our healing if we allow our past pains to imprison us. We must have faith and good works, according to James Chapter Two. The faith would be knowing to forgive ourselves and others, and good works would be getting forgiveness accomplished. An example of this would be saying, "I'll forgive, but I won't forget." The Word of God says that the fields are white with harvest, but the laborers are few. The reason the laborers are few is because faith will take you to the field, but it is the good works that gathers the harvest!

> Then He said to His disciples, The harvest is indeed plentiful, but the laborers are few. So pray to the Lord of the harvest to force out and thrust laborers into His harvest.

> Matthew 9:37-38, AMP

According to the Webster's dictionary, the word '*laborer*' is defined as a person who does unskilled physical work for wages. In other words, the laborers are few when it comes to the harvest of healings for ourselves to be healed and made whole. You can't give what you don't have! If you aren't healed, then you can't help others get healed, and this is why the laborers are few. This too explains why we grow weary trying to do good.

We have been taught that the field consisted of lost souls that needed salvation. This is true in a certain sense. Our soul man consists of our mind, will and emotions. The fields here are full of healed souls (minds, wills, and emotions), but the laborers are few. We assume that the souls that are in the field belong to others; in all actuality, the field is white with healings for our own souls, but the laborers are few. We must think of the field as being ready to harvest for ourselves and once we become whole, then we can help others find wholeness as well.

Why would the fields be white, if it consisted of lost souls? If you continue to think that the fields are white with harvest (souls of the lost), you will continue to feel hopeless and remain confused about the harvest of healing which is at hand. So many times when we hear the Word of God, we unconsciously begin to think of other people's brokenness rather than our own. It is easier to see someone else's issues, rather than our own! The field is ready to harvest! A farmer usually reaps his own

51

crops first, not his neighbors. If the neighbor needs help harvesting, then the Christian thing to do would be to go over and help. We must reap our own healing first, where we can then help others.

The Harvest of Healing is ready to be gathered, but people are physically, mentally, emotionally and financially trying to get others healed and remain broken themselves. If we remain broken, we remain stuck in our past, unable to walk free in our destiny. The pains of our past will keep us in bondage of regret, unforgiveness and resentment. We want to free ourselves and forgive ourselves (and all others) in order to move into the things in which we desire to come forth. We must create an outlet (in the natural) by way of repentance that enables the new to come forth like the dawning of the day. Darkness (past) has to release the dawning (present) for the exchange to take place. We have to release the darkness of our past wounds in order for the light of God's glory to break forth. As long as you have unforgiveness in your heart, you will be stuck in the pain of that past! Laborers that are stuck cannot reap the harvest that God has for them. Let's release the pains of our past that keep us from operating in the prosperity of our present. Your past can't compliment your future; so therefore, you must release it. If you don't, it has the power to complicate and confuse your present.

> Then shall your light break forth like the morning, and your healing (your restoration and the power of a new life) shall spring forth speedily; your righteousness (your rightness, your justice and your right relationship with God) shall go before you [conducting you to peace and prosperity], and the glory of the Lord shall be your rear guard.
>
> Isaiah 58:8, AMP

And the glory of the Lord shall be your rear guard! And the glory of the Lord shall be your rear guard!! And the glory of the Lord shall be your rear guard!!! We need to get this word embedded within our abilities to understand that the glory of the Lord God Almighty is our Ultimate Covering!!!! In other words, God has got our back. In order for God to have our backs, we must let go of the things that seem as if they still cover us (our past). If you allow your past to continue to cover you, then you will eventually succumb to the dread of "nothing will ever be different for me." Whatever you hide behind becomes your covering. Adam could not carry the covering of God and fig leaves at the same time. There must be an exchange in order for the new to come forth. We must remove the past thoughts of all of our faults and failures and make ourselves available for the renewing of our minds that come along with the carrying of God's glory. Remember we can't take His way and our way too.

We can't carry the glory of God and our past!

How Do I Release My Past?

You may say, "How do I release my past?" This is another step to getting over ourselves. We release our past one pain at a time. Give the Holy Spirit permission to begin bringing up these pains and as He brings them up, repent for the driving force behind the pain. Example:

Fear of Failure- Fear of failure would try to keep you from trying new things in life because you would be afraid that it would fail. This may be from a past trauma of failure that revisits you because of the need to be healed. It may be something that caused a very embarrassing moment in you that left you feeling inferior or easily intimidated. Whatever the cause, ask the Holy Spirit to bring it to your attention and to set you free from it. As you give Him permission to bring it up, your responsibility is to repent of the fear that it has brought in your life, and the debt is canceled to where you can now try new things and be confident and successful.

Let me give you a model prayer that works for everything:

Dear Heavenly Father,

I purpose and choose with my free will to repent for _____(identify the driving force behind your pain whether it is fear, rejection, abandonment, etc). I ask you to forgive me Lord for operating under these negative emotions as sin in my life. I cancel this debt in Jesus' name. Satan, I cancel your authority and all of your tormentors and I come out of agreement with you now. Holy Spirit, please heal my broken heart and speak your words of truth. (now just listen for Him to speak).

You might want to consider purchasing **"Biblical Foundations of Freedom"** by Art Mathias to learn how to identify these driving forces. You will never be free from anything that you cannot identify.

We might also want to repent for the way that we have controlled our lives to the point of almost destroying ourselves and others. We call ourselves being careful of others because we don't really know if they will hurt us or not. This is FEAR & CONTROL! Hello, is anybody home? Why are we protecting ourselves? We have been hurt so many times by others in the past that we don't want to risk being hurt again. When we *get over ourselves,* we cannot be offended! If someone hurts you, then it's your fault. Now wait a minute and don't get your feathers too ruffled. The brokenness inside of you, is what gets offended. When you are made whole, that's when whoever can say whatever and it won't effect you any longer. Glory to God!!!!

Being offended is a defense mechanism that kicks in to protect ourselves from experiencing pain. In all actuality, we need to rid ourselves of the pain through the process of forgiveness and release the past, so that the present will have a chance to be fruitful. Remember, it is time that we reap what Jesus has already sown: **"HEALING!"** I need my soul healed (mind, will & emotions) from my past, to walk in my destiny. You must release yourself, lean back on Him and be free.

If we continue to procrastinate this process of releasing our past, we will eventually become bitter. We hide ourselves behind the walls of false protection that we build up to keep us from getting hurt. The Word of God says to guard our hearts (not to dam them up), for out of them flow the issues of life. When things become dammed up, there will eventually be a time of bursting that will take place, and this is when you unconsciously hurt other people and don't even try to. This is also a place in the natural that invites heart attacks, strokes, high blood pressure, panic attacks, aneurysms, etc.

Medical doctors' first advice to such a diagnosis would be, "If you can control worry, then you could control this." Worry (stress) is based in fear and when fear is repented of, the worry has to flee!

The Lord ministered to me one time that He wanted me to go on a fast. I agreed and asked the Lord, *"What kind of fast?"* He said, *"Fast Worry!"* I said, *"Lord, I'm worried I can't do that."* I began the fast, and every thought that would arise that consisted of worry, I would repent of the thought and was released from the anxieties. It worked so much, that I fasted again the next day and it eventually became a way for me to live. I don't know a soul alive today that would rather **NOT** live worry free!!!

Don't WORRY!!!!!!!!!!

The Holy Spirit will expose things one pain at a time to you, and this will be the process that removes these pains layer by layer. Getting over ourselves is a daily chore. Be patient with yourself as this process comes forth. Remember, the pains have been there a long time, and it could take some time to deal with them one by one.

Some people have angrily said to me that once they received Christ as their Savior, He covered all of their pains. Well, this is true. Jesus did pay the price, but try telling that to your waitress the next time you go out to a restaurant. He did pay the price, and He has made a way that we could be set free, but we also have to pay the price as well. Fortunately, all we have to do is be willing to deal with our stuff and apply His blood (power) to our issues, and SHAZZAM, we can be made whole. You are really kidding yourself if you think that you have no part in this process. Daily repentance and forgiveness is a must in this process of being made whole for the glory of God.

Let me give you an example: The family joke that everyone around the dinner table always brings up at holidays and reunions. It's real easy to laugh when everyone else does. How do you really feel about that embarrassing moment when someone should have stuck up for you, but instead made a joke out of you that has lasted for years? If there are negative emotions or pains associated with a past event and/or with the people that were involved, then there needs to be forgiveness. Our brokenness allows our past to have power over our future!

You may say *"This is silly."* Is it? Did it leave you fearful in front of crowds or maybe insecure about your appearance? Take a moment to reflect and ask the Holy Spirit to show you the truth.

There is no place for your past in the present!

Dear Father,

I come to You and ask that You would forgive me for the way that I have held on to my past and tried to walk in newness at the same time. Please forgive me for the way that I sought comfort in holding on to my past pains. Lord, I give You permission to begin this process of renewal. Please give me revelation that will guide me through to see myself restored. I am ready to reap my healing. Help me not to worry and to have the faith that I need to walk in the wholeness that You have already made available to me. Forgive me for the way that I allowed my fears to control me and keep me in a place of bondage of my past. I release myself of all of my past chains that try to hold me captive, and I release myself to be free of my past, in Jesus' Name. Lord, I also forgive everyone that hurt me by always bringing up hurtful things at family gatherings. I also forgive myself for any way that I have operated under fear, rejection, and abandonment. I release myself now, in Jesus' Name.

Renovation Makes Room For Revelation

Early into my ministry, I began taking homeless teenagers into my home. I decided that if this was being established as part of my life, then I might as well purchase a large enough home to house the children. As I began looking for the right abode, I found an old house that was built in 1905. It was enormous and full of potential, but on the outside it looked as if it needed to be pushed over by a bulldozer. The house across the street from this monstrous structure was its twin, and by the way, it was eventually demolished.

When I stepped up onto the gorgeous but warped wrap-around porch I heard the voice of God say, *"This shall be called **The House of David**."* My natural father was standing beside me, and as I glanced over at him, he knew what the Lord was telling me and acknowledged it by shaking his head in a "NO" motion.

He said, *"Becky Lynn, it's going to take a lot of work."* I said, *"I know Daddy, but this shall be called **The House of David**."* This began a three year process of renovation. I didn't realize what my dad said was prophetic. This was an opportunity that the Lord had given me to be renewed alongside of this project. So many times we don't mind helping others find a place of renewal, it's just hard for us to do for ourselves. Little did I know God was showing me personally. As I began my renovation process on myself and the house, **it took a lot of work!** But the final product is glorious!!! Little did I know that as I renovated this old house, that I too would be made whole, along with others as well.

I immediately called the number on the real estate sign, and the agent that answered said, *"This is **David**. May I help you?"* It was hilarious

57

how many men by the name of David would be assigned to this project. The air-conditioning man, the man that delivered the furniture, the man that assembled the furniture, my backyard neighbor... We finally got to where when a new man would show up we would say, "Is your name David?" We have to look for signs, and not wonder how He will bring forth a miracle. The Word of God says that signs shall follow those who believe. This was another sign to me that God could and would fully support me in my endeavors concerning His children. Thank God for all of the Davids in the world (especially the ones that helped us)!

I met with David about the property and he quickly told me that someone else was interested. If I was serious, I needed a $15,000.00 earnest money deposit within seven days. As I look back now, I think David used that as a sales pitch! Then, the next question that he asked me was, *"How much do you have?"*

With this in mind, I asked him a few questions in return. The first question was, *"David, are you a believer?"* His response was, *"Why yes, I am."* Then he went on to explain to me that he was really involved with the youth ministry at his church. Saints, let me stop and explain something to you. It doesn't matter how much you are involved with at church, it matters how much faith you have when the rubber meets with the asphalt.

I said, *"Good."* The next question caught him off guard when I asked him could I borrow something. He tried to speak, but something came out of his mouth as a muffled stutter. I said, *"David, if you are a believer, and you are highly involved with your youth, then surely you have enough faith for me to borrow! I don't have the first dollar to put down on this house."* With a slight grin of relief on his face, he reassured me that I had a solid week to acquire the money.

David returned in four days to check up on me. When he entered my office, I said to him, *"David, I thought that you were a believer that worked with the youth group."* He nodded and said, *"I am."* I said,

"Well, you must not have much faith." He answered with a frown on his face, *"You weren't able to come up with the money, were you?"* I told him, *"I've only got $11,000.00, but I've still got three more days, too."* On the seventh day, David walked into my office and I had $15,000.00 ready to hand him for the earnest money that he had asked for.

I own a beauty salon and my customers love to hear all of my glory stories. Something was definitely different about that week. Every time I would tell about the old house that I had found, the people would write their checks for thousands over what their hair service was. **Glory to God!** Oh, and another thing I almost forgot, David advised me to be prepared to pay all of the closing costs on the home, because the bank had the home as a foreclosure, and refused to lose any more money on the property.

The day of the closing my attorney looked at me and asked me how did I do this, and I replied, *"Do what?"* He said, *"How did you convince the bank to pay all of the closing costs on this foreclosed property?"*

I smiled and said. *"This is God's house, not mine. That's how!"* That journey is another book within itself, and you can look for it in the near future. We were excited about the purchase of our "new/used" children's home that would be a refuge to many as they dealt with rejection and abandonment issues from their natural parents, and so the adventure began. We too are like this old house, broke down and nothing to work with, but God sees a palace within us, when all we might see is poverty.

We would come together every Saturday with willingness in our hearts and gloves on our hands as we prayerfully went into this seemingly impossibility to pull out the beauty from the ashes. The neighbor across the street later told me that she would watch as we gathered every Saturday morning in a prayer circle before we started our day. Little did she know that we were also praying for her. We had no idea that our prayers were being so honored, that Jesus healed her of cancer. The Lord ministered to me that as we renovated this piece of art, He would heal us from the inside out. Many people were healed mentally, physically and spiritually as they volunteered their time toward this project.

Renovation Is A Process

Renovation is like healing, it is a process like peeling an onion, you remove it layer by layer. First, we had to patiently chip away at the mortar that was on the walls with screw drivers and hammers. Removing all the mortar eventually posed another problem for us: as the mortar piled up, it formed a sandy substance that held a lot of weight. My father told me if I didn't do something quick with all of that mortar, the floors would began to sag. I checked into having it disposed and it was going to cost a small fortune because of the weight of it. I prayed and asked the Lord what to do, and He said to wait. That's not really what I wanted to hear. Sometimes what God tells you to do is at times opposite to the instructions of others, but He always knows best. I was sort of stuck in the middle of a rock and a hard place.

I continued to wait, reassuring my earthly father that I was taking care of the matter. One afternoon while working on the house, a man stopped by and ask me what I planned to do with all of that mortar. I quickly told him that I didn't have a clue as to what to do with it, and that's when he asked me if he could have it to fill in some holes on his farm. The children and I joyfully loaded his ton trailer up several times before getting it all out of the house. Thank God for answers to seemingly great dilemmas! One man's mess is another man's miracle.

We removed board by board from the walls and ceiling that made up the inside structure. Spiritually, I know now, that He had us to remove the walls within our hearts that we had built to keep everyone out. The ceiling was representation of the limits that had been placed over us. Remember, the Bible says to *"Guard your heart,"* not build up walls! (Prov. 4:23). Seemingly, the more we would remove, the bigger the mess became. I felt led to keep the half inch slats that held the mortar on the walls and later lined my prayer chamber with them; they created a beautiful wall covering for that room.

Another amazing factor about this project is that we never had a blueprint of what we were creating. We had the faith to believe that as we worked, God would show us exactly what to do and when to do it! This took a lot of faith because we really didn't have any knowledge of carpentry, but as long as we followed Him, we couldn't go wrong. The designs that we ended up with turned out to be heavenly. I have people ask me all of the time who designed our house. It's fun to tell them that we had a Master Designer.

Let this minister to you: when you begin to take the walls down from your heart, it will seem as if things are getting worse, not better. I want to encourage you: the mess is what God needs for you to surrender to Him, so He can turn it into your miracle. Allow your faith to work as the Master Designer creates this for you as well.

As we removed all the walls and the ceiling, the Lord ministered to me NOT to take away any of the load bearing walls. I first had to ask my earthly father what a load bearing wall was. A load bearing wall gives a building structural integrity. It carries and distributes weight from the roof and top floors down to the foundation. Damage to a load bearing wall can cause floors to sag, finishes to crack, and the entire structure to collapse. This is the single most important factor when beginning renovation.

Sound familiar to your christian walk? God equips us with the strength to hold up under all the pressures of humanity, but we false burden bear to the point that we always try to carry other people's burdens. This is when we begin to crack and collapse! We were not meant to carry people's burdens, we are meant to carry the cross (Matt. 16:24). God didn't allow our existence here on earth so that it overcomes us, but that we could overcome it (Rev. 2:7). Be real careful to protect the load bearing walls in your life.

False burden bearing is when we take on the emotional responsibilities of others. We assume that we can change other people's situations and/or conditions, not realizing the danger that we are putting ourselves in physically. **Note:** One that carries another's burdens emotionally, usually has chronic neck, shoulder and back pain. This can also cause curvature of the spine when children take on the responsibilities of their parent's issues. The answer to this healing would be to repent of false burden bearing, and ask God to forgive you for this act and then forgive yourself and then your pain has to flee. I've actually seen crooked spines of adults straighten out when they repented for false burden bearing.

Do you want me to lead you through this prayer?

Dear Heavenly Father,

I purpose and choose with my free will to repent for false burden bearing and I ask you to forgive me, Lord. I am not meant to carry other people's burdens. I cancel this debt in Jesus' Name. Amen

Take a good long deep breath, straighten up your back and see how that feels. You may have to pray this prayer daily if you normally take on other people's stuff. Your stuff is enough to break a camel's back, much less taking on other's!

YOUR STUFF IS ENOUGH!

How To Take "COURAGE" Out Of Discouragement

Diligence, dedication, and discouragement were the driving forces behind this project. Yes, I said **DISCOURAGMENT**. For the first time in my life, I learned from discouragement. Instead of discouragement getting me down, I used it as a footstool to take me higher. I found out that any time I do something courageous for the Lord, the enemy tries to discourage me. So any time discouragement comes forth, just take the courage from it and let the discouragement drive you to your destiny.

We do not own discouragement; it comes to affect, defect and influence our characteristics in Christ Jesus. Discouragement usually comes to cold-cock your Christianity and cause your faith to faint. We must beat the enemy at his own game. The more discouragement came, the more diligence and dedication stirred up within me. Instead of allowing discouragement to destroy me, I gave it permission to encourage me because I knew that it was going to be an incredible outcome. Have you ever heard the old saying, "If you can't beat them, join them?" The only way to beat the enemy is to agree with him quickly, then use whatever tactic he formed against you, to then destroy him (Matt 5:25).

I was very careful not to take anything away from the structure that was significant to the foundation. The foundation was great and the load bearing walls were secured. It all worked together to uphold this century-old residential skeleton.

We must be aware of pillars in our lives that God has established in us as truths, and no matter what the influence, never allow these pillars of truth to be removed. Counterfeit pillars are the emotions that affect us the most in a negative manner. We must remove these counterfeit pillars and replace them with good, strong, healthy pillars that will ensure a stable foundation.

Three-quarters of the way through this process of renovation, the enemy tried to steal my joy by hindering the supernatural flow of prosperity. I patiently waited on the finances that were necessary to complete this project. As I prayed, the attacks were at an all-time high, and God answered my prayers by way of a holy visitation. One day while working on the house, a few cars pulled up in the front yard and people began to walk around the property. I went out and introduced myself and one of the elderly people within the group asked me if she could get one of the original bricks from underneath the home. Suddenly, I realized that her passion for this place was familiar with that of mine.

I asked the group of strangers what their interest was in this property and two of the elders began to reminisce about their childhood experiences. They started by saying that the front room was the location of their birthing, along with the giggles of several "off the beaten path childlike stories." As my father and I stood in the foyer of the home, listening to their view of the past memories, I heard the Holy Spirit say to me that the prayers of their mother were still resounding in the halls of this home. I actually heard one of the prayers that said, *"Lord, please take care of the children."*

Their faces soon transitioned from the joy that they had been expressing, to somewhat of a sad countenance. They began by saying that the baby became sick with polio and the family (along with the neighbors) was sitting up in prayer for the baby's recovery, when suddenly, the young father fell dead with a massive stroke. This tragedy was a shock to the community, alongside the disease that struck the youngest of their six children. Becoming a widow at a young age and the worry of the baby's sickness, the mother a year later succumbed also to a premature death as she was rushed into the operating room hemorrhaging. The baby survived along with the other five children, who were all placed within the same orphanage in North Georgia.

By this time I could hardly keep all the tears wiped away from my eyes, when one of the original children who was now in her nineties, looked at me and asked me this question.

"Honey, What in the world are you going to do with this big 'ole house?"

I could hardly answer her, but it was then that I told her about our plans for a children's home that would house children that had undergone some of the same issues in which they had faced. **This visitation gave me enough confirmation that encouraged me to continue the renovation.**

Part of the renovation process was the addition of the upper level. Several people told me that I was not going to be able to add a second story, when God had already given me revelation on the layout.

Revelation can't be wrong! Don't ever allow anyone to steal your revelatory vision. Revelation is an answer to impossible situations.

Revelation Is The Answer To Impossible Questions

If you know in part what the Lord shows you, then prophesy in part. Remember, He will always confound the wise, by calling forth the foolish things (I Cor. 1:27). I knew that if I was going to add another story to this house, I was going to have to double-up on the foundation. In order to go higher, you must always first go wider and deeper. Your foundation has to go wider and deeper, if you're going to succeed in going up. If not, you will eventually experience a collapse that should have never taken place (kind of like a lot of Christians). I told my guys that between every pillar underneath the house, there had to be another pillar added; we had to double up on the foundation in order to achieve a higher level. So therefore, it was accomplished and we were able to add a second story with great success. *Hallelujah!*

> But seek (aim at and strive after) first of all His kingdom and His righteousness (His way of doing and being right), and then all these things taken together will be given you besides.
>
> Matthew 6:33, AMP

When you establish a good foundation in the Word of God, then you can go as high as you want to as the Lord adds unto you. The Bible says, *"Delight yourself also in the Lord, and He will give you the desires and secret petitions of your heart" (Ps. 37:4, AMP).* The Word of God also says to seek ye first the kingdom of God and all these other things shall be added unto you (even a second story). The sky is not even a limit for you! After a while, what started as renovation slowly turned into restoration by way of revelation. Revelation always births restoration. There came a point in this journey that once everything that needed to be removed was out, the new could begin its process of completion. The hardest part of the battle was ripping out the old to make room for the new! I was finally at the point that I could now began adding back to the structure. It looked empty, kind of like I felt!

"CHANGE"

I can tell you a quick story about one of the children that I took in. I was thirty-five and single and began to ask God about my life and that if taking in kids was my future, that I would be content doing this for the Kingdom. I also explained to Him that I would really like to name a little girl after myself because I carry my grandmother's name. I guess every woman dreams of naming her little girl after herself or her grandmother. The Lord answered me a little differently than I thought that He would (He usually does). Thank God, child-bearing wasn't in His equation. The fourth child that I took in had the same exact name as me, so I got my answer and my daughter named Rebecca Lynn. By the way, I have been the proud parent of sixteen children and growing. **GLORY TO GOD!**

NOTES:

CHAPTER 4

THE REST OF GOD

I was missing out on the one of the greatest aspects of God: His rest. Rest is the beginning of Restoration (ration of rest). You Have to rest in order to receive revelation. The reason I didn't have the revelation of God was because I wasn't resting in God. Rest brings forth revelation. The rest of God is also the peace of God. Why do we wait until we die to R.I.P.?

If you don't have rest, you don't have a nest for restoration to be stored. A mother bird has to prepare her nest before she can deliver her eggs. This preparation is compared to the preparation of restoration in God's children; there must be a place where the restoration is delivered a nesting place (this is also called "the secret place" in Ps. 91). The enemy would have us to be busy, so that this place could not be established within us. When we are constantly busy without resting, then we are setting ourselves up for an up-coming total disaster. Before I found this secret place in God, I would go a good, strong three or four months before collapsing and having to sleep twenty four to thirty hours to catch up. Eventually it got to where I could only go three or four weeks without collapsing again and having to sleep a couple of days to catch up. I was addicted to drivenness: having to be constantly busy, side-stepping my issues at hand. I side-stepped them because I didn't know how to deal with them!

B. U. S. Y. = Being under satan's yoke!

I've learned in my wholeness that I must reserve a place within myself in which God's peace can come (this is true intimacy) and surpass all my understanding. If we don't understand something, we need to consider changing positions to make a place for understanding! We need to repent for our misunderstanding (make room for understanding), because misunderstanding could be a lack of knowledge that ends up destroying you. You must have a place that you can get in, in order to receive true peace that comes along with restoration. The Word of God calls this, again, the secret place (Ps. 91).

The Secret Place Of God

Rest escorts you into homeostasis. Homeostasis is an ideal or virtual state of equilibrium, in which all body systems are working and interacting in an appropriate way to fulfill all the needs of the person and/or the body. Anytime you are sick, the doctor will order rest. The enemy wants to keep you away from this place because it is the place in which God blessed.

REST IS BLESSED

I have to remind myself every day to remain in this place of peace because if I don't, worry seeps in and causes fear. It's been stated that over eighty percent of sickness is due to the fear, stress and negative emotions that we allow to reside within. A good deep breath of fresh air is a good reminder to release your anxieties. When we are full of anxieties, we forget to breathe a full breath. When we are full of anxieties, we forget to live a full life. May we practice this exercise right now?

Take a deep breath, hold it and then exhale.

Take another deep breath, hold it and then exhale.

One more time, take a deep breath, hold it and then exhale.

BETTER?

And God blessed (spoke good of) the seventh day, set it apart as His own, and hallowed it, because on it God rested from all His work which He had created and done.

Genesis 2:3, AMP

And it shall be in that day that the Root of Jesse shall stand as a signal for the peoples; of Him shall the nations inquire and seek knowledge, and His dwelling shall be glory [His rest glorious]!

Isaiah 11:10, AMP

Thus says the Lord: Stand by the roads and look; and ask for the eternal paths, where the good, old way is; then walk in it, and you will find rest for your souls. But they said, "We will not walk in it!"

Jeremiah 6:16, AMP

So then, there is still awaiting a full *and* complete Sabbath-rest reserved for the [true] people of God. For he who has once entered [God's] rest also has ceased from [the weariness and pain] of human labors, just as God rested from those labors peculiarly His own. Let us therefore be zealous *and* exert ourselves *and* strive diligently to enter that rest [of God, to know and experience it for ourselves], that no one may fall *or* perish by the same kind of unbelief *and* disobedience [into which those in the wilderness fell].

Hebrews 4:9-11, AMP

In other words, the visions and creative miracles that God has for you to receive and/or give to others, can be found in a place of rest. God told Moses in the 33rd chapter of Exodus that *"My Presence shall go with you, and I will give you rest."* As long as we have God's Presence, we will have His rest. We cannot enter into His promise, if we don't first find His rest.

**You show me a tired, worn out, busted and disgusted
Christian and I will show you a "Christian
without His presence."**

Can we just stop right here and repent for being too busy?

Dear Heavenly Father,

*I purpose and choose with my free will to repent for always being
busy. Please forgive me for being so busy because I didn't know what to
do with myself. Help me Lord to deal with my stuff and find Your secret
place of peace and rest, in Jesus' Name.*

It also says in the next verse (15), *"And Moses said to the Lord, If Your
Presence does not go with me, do not carry us up from here."* We need
to get to the place that if God's Presence (His rest) doesn't carry us, then
we shouldn't try to go ourselves. It is in our time of weariness and
weaknesses that the enemy beats us up so bad and throws us out into the
streets like the seven sons of Sceva:

> And there were seven sons of *one* Sceva, a Jew, *and* chief of
> the priests, which did so. And the evil spirit answered and
> said, Jesus I know, and Paul I know; but who are ye? And the
> man in whom the evil spirit was leaped on them, and
> overcame them, and prevailed against them, so that they fled
> out of that house naked and wounded.

> Acts 19:14-16, KJV

Have you ever walked into a season of your life that seemed as if
everything that you touched became barren? It is because God's presence
(rest) did not accompany you on this journey. If you are a tired, worn-out,
busted and disgusted Christian, then ask yourself the question, *"where
have I been without the Presence and rest of God?"* We cannot afford to
go into places in life without God's Presence and rest going beside us.

70

God's presence has to be invited, and then you will become united with His peace that is always evidence of His presence (rest). God's revelation leads you to a place of rest, and rest escorts you on into restoration. Rest is opening yourself up to restoration.

God can't restore you in a rush. Convenience is not in the equation, but it does qualify you for the counterfeit. He is the rushing mighty wind that Acts Chapter 2 speaks of, "but He **RESTED** upon the people that day in the upper room." He will rush in and give you rest, but you cannot receive rest if you are in a rush!

> For since the beginning of the world *men* have not heard, nor perceived by the ear, neither hath the eye seen, O God, besides thee, *what* he hath prepared for him that waiteth for him.
>
> Isaiah 64:4, KJV

The enemy would have us to seek convenience in the natural, because Jesus has made eternity convenient for those who seek it. Convenience in the natural is contrary to spiritual convenience, though. Be real careful not to be deceived. We assume convenience is the best way, but in all actuality, convenience in the natural is expecting someone else to make things easier for us. Spiritual convenience, on the other hand, is trusting and believing that He has created a way where there seems to be no way for us and waiting on that way to come to pass.

The Webster's dictionary defines '*convenience*' as "something conducive to comfort or ease." Convenience (in the natural) is usually a temporary fix. We want convenience because we don't want to wait. But, it's in the place of wait that we see God more clearly. The wait period is God's way of encouraging us to rest. This is the time that our faith finds peace to rest and as we rest, time passes us by, producing eternal promises (miracles). Things change in the process of WAIT.

Convenience is the platform for complaints!

71

Time as we know it is opposite to eternity simply because time is limited. Eternity is not limited! When eternal promises come forth, time as we know it has to bow in reverence to eternity because it is the greater power. This is what we call "Heaven invading Earth," therefore causing humanity to WAIT as the process takes place. The word of God speaks often about waiting upon the Lord:

> But they that wait upon the Lord shall renew their strength; they shall mount up with wings as eagles; they shall run, and not be weary; and they shall walk, and not faint.
>
> Isaiah 40:31, KJV

> I waited patiently and expectantly for the Lord; and He inclined to me and heard my cry.
>
> Psalm 40:1, AMP

The Bible refers to this place as **"a secret place."**

> HE WHO dwells in the secret place of the Most High shall remain stable and fixed under the shadow of the Almighty [Whose power no foe can withstand].
>
> Psalm 91:1, AMP

We must learn to dwell in His rest. The GLORY must have a place reserved to reside. Example: The widow in the Bible had to have containers to store the oil that was coming to her as provision (2 Kings 4). She had to WAIT as heaven invaded earth to bring forth a manifested miracle. While she was waiting, she also had to have the faith which provided containers for the glorious provisions that was being delivered. We must have our container ready and rested to receive the power for ourselves and others. We must reserve a place within us that the glory of God can reside. God's GLORY will always come to bring forth provisions. God is PRO-vision, not anti-vision *"according to His riches in GLORY" (Phil. 4:19).* Your availability to rest establishes a place, and your faith invites the glory to come, and as you wait in His presence, this

72

is the place where miracles come forth. If you are struggling with lack of provision, quit blaming God for your lack, and get into a place where you make room for His provision to come forth, then stand back, rest, wait and watch Him work. We need to adapt to the mentality of waiting because this is the place of renewal!

Here is an example: quit complaining about what you don't have. Start acknowledging and praising Him for what you do have, and you will make room for Him to supply more. I learned this lesson from God when I cleared some land to put a home on it. I didn't have the money to sow grass seeds or buy sod. I didn't even have enough money to buy a lawn mower, even if I did have grass! I would borrow my father's lawn mower every week and mow my weeds. The Lord assured me if I would praise Him for the grass that I couldn't see in the natural, He would bring it forth in the Supernatural. From the road, mowed weeds look like a manicured yard!

Just because something isn't working YET for us doesn't mean that it won't ever work. It may be waiting on our faith to bring it forth. I was diligent and steadfast in mowing my weeds faithfully every week without hesitation or dread. Eventually, the grass seeds that were on the deck of my father's mower (when borrowed to mow my weeds) would fall on my land that was prepared in expectation of what could be, took root, and spread to a full yard of green covering. Now I have so much grass, I can hardly keep it all mowed! We must be faithful in the small things in order to be blessed with more.

The Bible says,

> "May He grant you out of the rich treasury of His glory to be strengthened and reinforced with mighty power in the inner man by the [Holy] Spirit [Himself indwelling your innermost being and personality]."
>
> Ephesians 3:16, AMP

God wants to bless us with more, but our brokenness will not allow these blessings to come forth. We must allow God to strengthen (heal) our inner man to equip us with a kingdom mentality. It is our inner man that is weakened by past pains and regrets. God wants to pour Himself out upon us, but we must be able to contain His power in order to give it to others.

You can't give what you don't have!

I gathered from the passage of 2 Kings 4 that there was a lesson to be learned from borrowing these vessels from the widow's neighbors. Apparently, they had already run out of oil and had no need for the vessels any longer. Emptiness is the evidence of not being available for true intimacy. Emptiness is also the evidence of busyness. Normally, if the neighbor thought that he would have need of this container, surely he would have kept it for himself. Usually, a neighbor won't hesitate to let another borrow a cup of milk; just don't ask for the gallon!

If you have recently run out of resources, don't give up, stay in position, because overflow is on its way. Get yourself healed so that when the provisions do come ,you will be able to contain them. In other words, the neighbors had no desire to keep an empty vessel, but spiritually, we know that emptiness comes right before OVERFLOW. *Hallelujah!!!!!!!!!*

I heard a story one time about an interview that took place between a reporter and a rail yard foreman. The interviewer asked the foreman, *"How can you identify the empty railway carts from the full ones that come down the railway?"* The foreman replied, *"Oh, that's easy. The empty ones make the most noise!"*

Emptiness will always come before
OVERFLOW!

This is going to make the biggest difference in our lives as believers in this present-day economic downfall. We will be the *"lender and not the borrower" (Deut. 15:6).*

I would have loved to have been there the day the widow gave the containers back to her neighbors full of oil that would never run dry. The lesson that I think the widow may have learned is true intimacy with the Father as her provider (husband). And then, she in return could give to others out of her overflow. Remember, we can't give something that we don't have.

You can't love your neighbor, if you don't love yourself!

We must recognize our emptiness as an opportunity to receive God's GLORY, which is His provision and peace. If the nest of emptiness is already established, let's just rest in His presence and believe that He will make a way where there seems to be no way. The Word of God says:

> But seek (aim at and strive after) first of all His kingdom and His righteousness (His way of doing and being right), and then all these things taken together will be given you besides. So do not worry or be anxious about tomorrow, for tomorrow will have worries and anxieties of its own. Sufficient for each day is its own trouble.
>
> Matt. 6:33-34, AMP

The only difference in emptiness and overflow is obedience.

Do you have room for provision and peace? Can I get someone to say, *"AMEN?"* We cannot be an old wineskin trying to contain new wine (Luke 5:37-39). We must find the place where we trade in the old, tired, worn-out, disgusted, busted, and broke repetitive way of thinking about our lives. We need to be renewed with the revelation of, we are a "NEW" creation in Christ Jesus. We must be restored to carry the glory of the

Lord. Our brokenness comes from our natural man that is made from the dust of the earth. Be real careful not to treat yourself like dirt just because you were made from it.

If you see yourself as dirt, you will treat yourself like dirt.

> Therefore if any person is [ingrafted[in Christ (the Messiah) he is a new creation (a new creature altogether); the old [previous moral and spiritual condition] has passed away. Behold, the fresh and new has come!

> 2 Corinthians 5:17, AMP

We must have our vessels ready. The Glory of God can only be contained if the vessel has been made whole. Sometimes that consists of trading the old in because it cannot be patched up. We must trade in our old way of thinking about ourselves and make room for the new way of thinking to bring forth the newness of Christ Jesus. The newness of Christ Jesus requires the newness of your mind-set. You can't contain something new in an old container.

> And no one pours new wine into old wineskins; if he does, the fresh wine will burst the skins and it will be spilled and the skins will be ruined (destroyed). But new wine must be put into fresh wine skins.

> Luke 5:37-38, AMP

Go with me on this scriptural journey for just a moment and let's see what God has for us to find. By the way, if you are all right with yourself, you may want to skip this section.

This next section is for the those who are "sick of themselves!"

How To Be Healed From Being Sick of Yourself

Self-Bitterness, self-hatred and self-judgments are all afflictions caused by negative emotions that will cause an unloving spirit to operate in your life. These emotions will cause you to become bitter towards not only yourself, but others as well. As this unloving spirit operates within us, it will eventually breed hardness and unforgiveness that will lead us into a place of resentment. This form of resentment also involves envy and jealousy that leaves one feeling empty and alone. One example of an unloving spirit is being around many people who truly love you, but yet you still feel unloved. It can also be identified as an orphan spirit. This condition refuses to let you love or be loved.

I found myself in this place two years ago, only to realize that I needed deliverance more than the people that I had been praying for. I began having symptoms of muscle soreness, low grade temperatures, and a feeling of continuous fatigue. Many people said that this sounded like symptoms of fibromyalgia and/or chronic fatigue syndrome. My life at thirty-eight felt as if I were eighty-eight! Not to mention the confusion that bombarded my very being. I couldn't make clear decisions about important matters. I was very concerned that I was losing my marbles.

The fact of the matter was that I had so much self-bitterness, self-hatred and self-judgment that it caused my mind to line up with the judgments that had been placed against it (negative emotions cause judgment). If I had the thought of how lazy I was, then my mind and body lined up with fatigue (that came from drivenness). I say this because busyness was one of the ways in which I felt worthy. If I didn't constantly stay busy, I felt unworthy. The fatigue also came in from hours of overtime I put in so I wouldn't look like a financial failure. In all actuality, I couldn't afford to stop because I felt as if I couldn't deal with myself, so I stayed busy with everything else. If I had negative emotions of how crazy most of my ideas were, then my mind became confused. If I had negative emotions of how terrible my body looked, then my muscles became sore. We have got to be aware of how we *feel* about ourselves, because that is how we will *feel*.

In the meanwhile, an extra exhaustion that I had was trying to look like I had it all together when really I was dying inside. *Can anyone relate?* This was all self-afflictions (auto-immune) brought on by my allowance of being against myself.

I had made myself sick, from being sick of myself!

Rebecca King

The Word of God says:

> What shall we then say to these things? If God be for us, who can be against us?
>
> Romans 8:31, KJV

I didn't need for the enemy to attack me, I was attacking myself. It probably would be a good idea to take some self-defense classes to learn how to protect ourselves from ourselves! We need to pay close attention not to blame the enemy for the things that we bring against ourselves. If we assume that the enemy is at fault, then the chances of our repentance are slim. Remember when we place blame on others, then we won't take responsibility for ourselves. As long as we can blame others, we will not take the responsibility of repentance, either. Repentance always brings forth restoration. If we blame the enemy for things that we have caused ourselves, there will be no answer for the questions that remain unanswered.

Peace is not present when unanswered questions remain!

I'll give you an example. A minister told me one time that she had a problem with anger and rage. She told me that she had been delivered from this anger and rage, but it would come back up from time to time. It was obvious to me as she was speaking about her rage that she wasn't

78

delivered. The rage still had a strong hold on her as she described her actions and reactions. She told me that when it would manifest she would say, "Satan get behind me, in Jesus name." I courageously looked at her and asked her if I could speak some truth over her, and she agreed. I said, "You have not been delivered." She looked at me like I had three eyes and two heads. I said again, "You haven't been delivered from this anger and rage, because every time that it manifests, you blame it on the devil and tell him to get behind you. You have to take accountability for your actions and reactions and get over yourself instead of satan getting behind you." This made perfect sense to her, and I led her through some repentance prayers and the Lord set her free.

The next time that anger and rage tries to come up, she knows to repent for the emotions that would enable them to manifest and live a life of freedom. We must take responsibility for our sins and quit blaming them on the devil. Who wants the devil behind them anyway, I want him under my feet!!! Why should we tell the devil to get behind us when he is supposed to be under us?

The Reason That I Was Getting Worse!

One afternoon while lying in the floor with one of my children, I realized my physical condition: it was painful to sit up for very long at a time. I then realized that I was getting worse and the only way that I knew that it could get any better was to address it spiritually. I began to consider my ways of why my condition was in this situation and wondered what I had done so wrong to be experiencing so much pain. In all actuality, it was what I had done to myself that caused so much pain. I repented for the way that I had treated myself and suddenly there was change. A little bit of repentance brought a whole lot of healing, so I began to dig a little deeper. I found out that the way I had treated myself actually became a part of me!

A little bit of repentance brought a whole lot of healing.

> You offspring of vipers! How can you speak good things when you are evil (wicked)? For out of the fullness (the overflow, the superabundance) of the heart the mouth speaks.

Matthew 12:34, AMP

I want to think of myself as a son or daughter of the Most High God would, not as an offspring of a viper. We don't realize that when we have negative thoughts about ourselves and do not repent of these thoughts, they linger within the walls of our minds. These thoughts eventually seep out of our mouths, producing afflictions that will soon break us down physically, mentally, emotionally and spiritually.

When we speak against ourselves, we are speaking evil about God's creation. We need to re-evaluate ourselves, considering the good instead of always analyzing our weaknesses. If you constantly focus on your weakness, then eventually you will fall prey to continual condemnation. We must realize what is in our heart before we can repent of it. We can't afford to have a Pharisaic (acting like a Pharisee) attitude about our own heart's issues. We must clean the inside of the cup (heart) and not only the outside. We must search out our own heart's issues because they are desperately wicked. Let's look at what Genesis says about the heart:

> And God saw that the wickedness of man was great in the earth, and that every imagination of the thoughts of his heart was only evil continually.
>
> Genesis 6:5, KJV

When I began my process of healing a few years ago, I would pray that God would fix my heart. I came to realize, over a period of seeking wholeness, that my heart was so broken and in need of life, I actually had to trade it in. My heart was so full of holes that it couldn't contain what God had to give me, that's why it felt full on Sunday after being in a good service and empty on Monday. I had to have a new container before I could have it pressed down, shaken together and overflowing.

Repentance brings renovation that produces restoration and cleanses (or either replaces) the hardness of our hearts. This process prepares us for overflow.

> Judge not, and ye shall not be judged: condemn not, and ye shall not be condemned: forgive and ye shall be forgiven: Give, and it shall be given unto you; good measure, pressed down, and shaken together, and running over shall men give into your bosom. For with the same measure that ye mete withal it shall be measured to you again.
>
> Luke 6:37-38, KJV

I had judged myself, so therefore, I caused a curse to come on my life of bitterness, hatred and judgment, which caused an unnecessary amount of emptiness.

Repentance will always bring restoration.

As I repented, I made myself available for a "brand new heart" from God. But first I had to be willing to let my old heart go.

> A new heart will I give you and a new spirit will I put with in you, and I will take away the stony heart out of your flesh and give you a heart of flesh.
>
> Ezekiel 36:26, AMP

I have a friend who went to pray for a lady who was in the hospital for a heart transplant, and he asked her what was wrong with her heart. (He had gone to visit as a favor for a friend. Obviously, he didn't personally know the lady.) She proceeded to tell him about the wilting of her heart that would soon bring death if not resolved.

What is wrong with your heart?

He asked her again, *"What's wrong with your heart?"* By this time, I'm sure the lady was wondering who this character was. She began to explain to him again what her diagnosis was. He stopped her and said, *"Who was it that hurt you so badly that it broke your heart?"* She began to weep and he was able to pray with her. The next day she called him and excitedly explained that the pre-op tests had come back, and her heart had totally restored itself! They released her from the hospital a day before what would have been the day for her heart transplant. Can we say, "RESTORATION?"

So don't be surprised if that transplant happens for you too (remember transfers have to happen before transplants). Maybe you need to reconsider praying for God to fix your heart, and go ahead and give him permission to just give you a brand **NEW** one. You are the vessel and God's GLORY wants to make you whole just as He did the woman with the issue of blood and the woman at the well.

No one is left behind in God's GLORY: man, woman, boy or girl. Red, yellow, black and white, we are all precious in His sight. God wants us all healed and made whole so that we can carry His glory that will illuminate the darkness that resides within this world. Let's get healed so that we can be a glory carrier!

Desolation comes after restoration to take you into
a place of visitation and on to your destination;
desolation is not your destiny! Don't be fooled by desolation.

Dear Heavenly Father,

I just want to say Thank You for the rest and peace that You have already provided for me. I repent for all of the ways that I have neglected this blessed place that You prepared especially for me to enjoy. Forgive me Father for serving the god of busyness to fulfill my longing to be accepted. Forgive me for all of the places that I have walked in my life that I didn't allow Your presence to walk with me. I release myself by way of repentance to receive restoration. I also repent for all the ways that I have sought convenience, and in return, this caused me to be full of complaints. I bless my inner man to receive the healing which is at hand that I may outwardly express Your wholeness. I forgive myself for not being able to love myself; therefore I could not love others. I also desire for You to teach me how to see myself as You see me. I have seen myself through my eyes of brokenness for so long that I don't even know who You created me to be. Help me to release the old and make plenty of room for the new to introduce me to my destiny for Your glory. Thank You Father for Your eternal plan of forgiveness. In Jesus' Name.

NOTES:

NOTES:

CHAPTER 5

DESOLATION IS NOT YOUR DESTINATION

This time in my life was the most desolate time that I had ever experienced, but I somehow knew that this was my last opportunity to finally be free. When desolation comes, don't procrastinate your deliverance. The renovation process that brought renewal and restoration to me was to ready me for my destination. My destiny had been put on hold because of the dysfunctional detours in my life. My procrastination wasn't intentional, it was because I didn't know how to get free. I wanted to be free and experience the peace and joy that I read about in the Word of God, but I didn't know how to get there.

Lack of knowledge will not only destroy you, but it will also keep you in a prison of fear as well. I felt like Moses on the back side of the wilderness in a place called Horeb (Ex. 3). Horeb is a place of visitation, it is not a state in which one is stuck. The enemy has tried to convince you that you are horrible and the place that you are in is horrible, but you are just visiting Horeb! Let's just continue through this place in which we thought that we would never survive and come out on the other side and thrive.

The Hebrew meaning for '*Horeb*' is "desolate." In other words, this was a place where Moses ended up tending the flock of his father-in-law as a profession; but this was not his destiny. Desolation is not our destiny! Moses was actually operating out of the fear of his past that held him captive from his future. Desolation comes when we have allowed things to hinder our destiny. Part of his destiny consisted of going back to the place of childhood and facing his enemy. In this instance, his enemy was not Pharaoh; his enemy was himself. He was running from who he had become! He was found at the well of decision, (Ex. 2:15) and instead of **getting over himself**, he chose to go with man's plan, and because of that, it took him an extra forty years to hear the Lord.

Has it seemed like years since you have heard the Lord? When you end up always doing for others and not dealing with your own stuff, it will feel as if you don't have a destiny. How many years have you invested in others that prolonged finding your own destiny? This process of procrastination will keep you in a lifetime of weariness and confusion.

Desolation is not your destiny!

Desolation doesn't drive you to your destination; visitation from God drives you to your destination. Desolation is a manifestation of destruction that invites an empty life. Desolation is the last place visited before you succeed or fail. It is a distraction from the enemy to steal your purpose in life. It is the deserted place, when we were created for the garden. One definition that Webster's dictionary holds for 'desolation' is "lifeless." We have to realize that our way is lifeless. The way others would have us to do things could end up lifeless as well, but God's way will always bring forth life.

Moses ended up at the well broken and in need of wholeness. How many times have we ended up at this place in life that we neglected to go on through and stayed broken because we didn't know what else to do? Here is good news my friend: you no longer have to live in the desert of desolation! Wholeness brings life, and His way brings life more abundantly (John 10:10). Don't give up in your place of desolation, because your destiny is undergoing a photosynthetic process. We will talk more about this later in Chapter Eight.

As the light of God's glory comes down and transforms you, you become your destiny. If we want to be set free from ourselves, we must look at ourselves face-to-face before we can be changed. *Glory*

Hallelujah!!! Our destiny doesn't consist of fulfilling someone else's dreams! Don't stop seeking your destiny just because you got caught up for years tending to someone else's business.

Let's see what the Word of God says:

> Do not be conformed to this world (this age), [fashioned after and adapted to its external, superficial customs], but be transformed (changed) by the [entire] renewal of your mind [by its new ideals and its new attitude], so that you may prove [for yourselves] what is the good and acceptable and perfect will of God, even the thing which is good and acceptable and perfect [in His sight for you].
>
> Romans 12:2, AMP

If you want to go up in your faith level concerning restoration, you must first be willing to go down. I know that sounds contrary, but the law of gravity says that what goes up, must come down (this is in the natural). In the supernatural, it is opposite. In order to go up, you must first go down. Pride will force you to go higher.

Humility instructs you to lower yourself.

> Pride *goeth* before destruction and a haughty spirit before a fall.
>
> Proverbs 16:18, KJV

> But many *that are* first shall be last; and *the* last *shall be* first.
> Matthew 19:30, KJV

> A man's pride will bring him low, but he who is of a humble spirit will obtain honor.
>
> Proverbs 29:23, AMP

Pride Disqualifies You From Receiving Spiritual Gifts

If the pride of life offers you an opportunity of elevation in this world, then this would explain it to be the counterfeit in which God desires for our lives. The Lord told me in order to go as high as you desire to go, you must first go down. Before Jesus ascended into heaven, the Word clearly states that He went into the lower parts (Eph. 4:9). The Word of God says that if we will *"Humble ourselves, then He would hear us from heaven and heal our lands."*

> If My people, who are called by My name, shall humble themselves, pray, seek, crave, and require of necessity My face and turn from their wicked ways, then will I hear from heaven, forgive their sin, and heal their land.
>
> 2 Chronicles 7:14, AMP

I asked the Lord to explain to me what the word *"land"* meant in this scripture. He began by telling me that it was *"everything,"* which didn't mean anything to me. As time went by and I sought His face, He revealed what *"everything"* was. I will be talking about this later in Chapter Twelve.

You must be willing to step down from what you know to be understanding, and make yourself available for His understanding. Our thinking is different from His thinking, and we must be willing to excuse our thoughts for His. Remember, the Word of God says that *"Our thoughts and His thoughts are different, for His are much higher."* We must look down into the well of our lives and see ourselves where we are and identify with the brokenness that is within us before we can seek a change.

You are greater than gravity!

> For My thoughts are not your thoughts, neither are your ways
> My ways, says the Lord. For as the heavens are higher than
> the earth, so are My ways higher than your ways and My
> thoughts than your thoughts.

Isaiah 55:8-9, AMP

His Word says, *"Lean not on your own understanding, but to acknowledge Him in all of His ways, and He would direct our paths" (Prov. 3:5-6 Author's paraphrase).* We have leaned on our own understanding so long, that we automatically assume that the way that we think is the right way. Unfortunately, a good majority of the things that I had always leaned on, I found out to be my brokenness. If I have learned anything in the past 24 months, it is that I really didn't know as much as I thought I did (when you can admit this, this is humility). If you think that you have always got to be in control and that your way is always the best way, you might want to repent of pride.

I even repented to God for acting like I always had it together, even when I didn't. I spent so much time trying to prove to others that I wasn't lacking in any area of intelligence, that I actually missed out on a lot of knowledge. Remember, Jesus is not a Bully, He is gentle and meek in His affairs. False intimacy and self-bitterness will convince you that you have to prove your knowledge to others, so you will feel better about yourself. This is hypocritical!

The Webster's dictionary defines '*hypo*' as "less than normal" and the word '*critical*' is defined as "inclined to criticize severely and unfavorable." In other words, when we become hypocritical, it is because we have criticized ourselves (and/or others) to the point that we feel less than unfavorable. Pride causes one to become a hypocrite. Be careful of this scheme, repent and be made whole. Being critical is not something that we were born with; it was learned from our brokenness.

Be careful not to be hypocritical.

Pride will tell you that you just can't look foolish in front of people, but the Word of God says, *"He would take the foolish things and confound the wise" (I Cor. 1:27).* Self-bitterness is also part of a broken heart. To research more about self-bitterness, I suggest that you read **Biblical Foundations of Freedom** by Dr. Art Mathias. He was the one who ministered to the woman at the hospital when God gave the lady a new heart. For you skeptics, that was nine years ago, and the lady is still alive!

The Webster's dictionary defines '*restoration*' as "an act of restoring or the condition of being restored; a bringing back to a former position or condition: REINSTATEMENT: RESTITUTION." When we realize what it is that the enemy has taken from us, then we will be able to take authority and command that he return it sevenfold.

> But if he is found out, he must restore seven times [what he stole]; he must give the whole substance of his house [if necessary---to meet his fine].
>
> Proverbs 6:31, AMP

That would be with interest and penalties! We first have to realize the degree of our brokenness to realize what we have need of. You have to know where you are to figure out where you are going. You also have to know what has been stolen in order to demand it returned. We have defended our brokenness for such a long time, because our pride didn't want to admit our feelings of failure, to the point that we have missed our healing because of our haughtiness.

**Pride comes in many forms; don't be
deceived by its
appearance.**

We had some items stolen from the children's home, and the police wanted to begin an investigation. They proceeded to ask me what the serial numbers were of my possessions. I looked at him as if the possibilities of his knowing the serial numbers of my possessions were greatly higher than that of mine. The serial numbers are symbolic of the identity of the stolen items in this investigation. In all actuality, we don't even know our own identity as a child of the Most High, therefore how do we demand an investigation of what the enemy has taken from us? The enemy finds it very humorous when we demand that he return items that we cannot even identify. We don't have the right to take back what we can't identify.

We must know our identity in Him.

We don't realize the importance of our identities in Christ Jesus. We first have to know who we are in Christ Jesus to line up with what has been stolen that we must take back from the enemy. We have to recognize our area of brokenness before we demand that the enemy return it. We haven't taken the necessary time to analyze ourselves as Jesus sees us. In fact, we have sympathized with ourselves in our bitterness and blamed it on others, and that in return has kept us in bondage to our fears of failure. We don't really know who we are in Christ (our true identity).

True intimacy with the Father brings forth our true identities. If we would invest as much time seeking our wholeness, rather than being available to the accusations the enemy speaks to us, we would see more of Him and less of ourselves (John 3:30). We become aware of our weaknesses to the point of hopelessness (which amplifies everything), but when we are made whole, we become more aware of His strength. In our weakness, He makes us strong (2 Cor. 12:9). We spend so much time defending our brokenness that we don't give our healing a chance to prove itself. When we are afraid to let go of our fears, we never give ourselves a chance to operate.

True intimacy with the Father brings forth our true identities.

Serving False Thoughts

Be careful in this process not to serve the gods of false thoughts. The Lord gave me a good scenario of this in I Kings 18, when Elijah went up against 850 false prophets calling down the fire of God. The ratio was 850 to 1. The false prophets, according to the numbers, were sure to win. Elijah mocked the gods and false prophets that swore that their god would perform. When nothing happened, they began to cut themselves in dismay.

The Lord showed me that this is true in our thought life. In the same way, the enemy comes against us with negative emotions, fears, doubts, and unbeliefs. Normally, we have one positive thought to every eight-hundred and fifty negative thoughts. Too many times, we fall prey to the false gods of negativity and discouragement. This is when we cut ourselves with negative emotions to the point of depression, and blame God for not showing up. The Word of God says, *"if you are going to serve Baal, serve Baal, but if not, serve God."* We need to be aware of these false thoughts that come to steal the fire of God from burning the impurities out of our negative emotions.

In verse 40 of this same chapter, Elijah seized all of the false prophets; not one of them escaped. We must take on Elijah's mentality when it comes to false thoughts and destroy every one of them without any of them getting away. In the next chapter, Elijah ended up under a juniper tree, dealing with his own fears that drove his self-pity. We must realize as children of God when we call the fire of God down to demonstrate His power to others, we must be prepared for His power to change us as well. What's good for the goose is also good for the gander.

These false thoughts will try to encourage us to protect our weaknesses to the point of actual promotion. What you don't deal with now, will deal with you, or maybe even your children later. We can't expect our children to deal with their brokenness if we don't deal with our own. If we continue to put off getting free from our issues, then we will eventually teach our children out of our brokenness.

Many times we justify our brokenness by saying that we are just protecting ourselves, but the more walls that you build to protect yourself, the more walls you are behind, hiding from God's healing. When you feel bombarded by your emotions, it is because you have backed yourself up into a corner of your own circumstances. Come out and be healed today!

What is BROKENNESS?

Brokenness is anything that keeps you from God's wholeness. Brokenness is also residues left within the walls of your heart from past pains---cracks that were created in your heart over time that convinced you that your brokenness could not be overcome.

Webster's defines '*brokenness*' as "violently separated as two parts: SHATTERED: CRUSHED: BANKRUPT; not complete or full." Not complete or full is what I was before the glory of God healed me. I've heard many Christians say that we just have to deal with the things that have happened to us in our lives and consider that God allowed these things to form us to be who we are. We live in a dark world and bad things do happen to good people, but when these bad things happen, it doesn't mean that we have to stay broken.

Brokenness is the effect of sin, and wholeness is the effect of healing. I don't know a person alive that hasn't experienced brokenness; they just don't know what to call it, so they just get accustomed to operating around it and call it life. Throughout our lives we experience situations and circumstances that leave us full of fear, rejections and abandonment. Fear opposes our faith, rejection steals our appetite for acceptance and abandonment is the ultimate betrayal. We must identify our brokenness as a foreign object and reject it in order to receive the fullness of God's promises before His plans can promote our purposes. We need His wholeness to replace our brokenness.

You might ask the question, *"What is brokenness?"* Here are a few examples of the brokenness in our lives that keep us from our wholeness.

Examples of Brokenness:
- Unforgiveness in our hearts from past hurts
- Bitterness from being betrayed
- Fear of people and their opinions
- Fear of failure
- Insecurities
- Resentments
- Judgments
- Rejections
- Ridicules
- Fear of being real and people rejecting you
- Fear of trying new ways
- Not feeling loved
- Unable to express yourself
- Fear of Conversations or Communication
- Fear of Intimacy
- Fear of not being heard
- Fear of ourselves
- Fear of fear

Remember, brokenness is anything that keeps you from God's wholeness. I highly recommend that you get a piece of paper and write down some of your own brokenness that has kept you from your wholeness and possibly your destiny. If you just had the thought that this is crazy and I'm not doing this exercise: Excuse me, but you are the one who needs it the most.

Procrastination is the putting off of your destination.

Three Steps To Overcoming Brokenness

Jesus says in Mark 14:22 AMP, *"And while they were eating, He took a loaf [of bread], praised God and gave thanks and asked Him to bless it to their use. [Then] He broke [it] and gave to them and said, Take. Eat. This is My body."* We have to learn that instead of partaking in our brokenness, we must partake and eat of His body which was broken for us to be made whole. We must not live by bread alone but by every Word that God has spoken concerning our healing. We must abide in the constant communion that Jesus made Himself available to us in order for us to live in our wholeness.

My four year old son reminds us every time that we sit down to eat, that we need to take communion. What a blessing to understand at such a young age that we have this advantage over our brokenness. We had a religious guest over for dinner one night and Eli asked if anyone wanted to take communion. The guest was surprised that he even knew what communion was (it's not usually what a four year old talks about at dinner). The guest agreed that he wanted to partake of communion and my son tore him off a piece of bread and handed it to him. The guest questioned my son about what the piece of bread meant and my son quickly responded, "It's Jesus' body."

We have to realize that Jesus died that we could have life and life more abundant, so therefore, the areas in our lives that have died, can live again. The brokenness that keeps us from our wholeness has to be traded in once and for all. Brokenness leaves us empty, and wholeness keeps us in overflow.

1. We must be "Hungry for our Healing."
2. We must be "Willing to try His way over our own."
3. Relate our present condition with our past brokenness and realize that we need His strength to make us "WHOLE."

When you come hungry and willing, you will be made WHOLE.

We have to remember what Jesus did for us. First, we have to receive the bread of life as nourishment and then as a symbol of the resurrection power of healing. The hardest part of healing and being restored is the acknowledgment of our need to be healed (the opposite of pride is humility). Your pride will tell everyone that you are alright, when you are really wilting inside. Pride is evidence of your brokenness being offended. Humility causes a hunger, and hunger craves fulfilling. We must become hungry for Him before He can fill us. Pride will keep you empty and on the outskirts of your healing. You will be able to see it, but will not be able to reach it.

Secondly, we need the willingness that it takes to receive the power to be healed. The woman with the issue of blood had tried every avenue to be healed; she tried everything that she thought would do the trick. She ran out of resources as she sought professional opinions, as well as blaming herself for her afflictions. One exhausted day, she put it all together and realized that what she had put her faith in wasn't getting the job done (Mark 5:25-34).

We put our time and effort towards other things and people, only to end up exhausted and still empty. Then we blame ourselves and others for the lack of healing and become bitter. When we blame others for our lack of healing, we become full of judgment and unforgiveness.

It was prophesied in the book of Isaiah in the 53rd chapter that *"He was wounded for our transgressions, He was bruised for our guilt and iniquities; the chastisement, peace and well-being for us was upon Him, and with the stripes that wounded Him we are made WHOLE."* In other words, He allowed Himself to become broken, so that we could be made whole.

Fear makes us vulnerable to brokenness.

Fear makes us vulnerable to brokenness. God doesn't give us the *"spirit of fear" (2 Tim. 1:7)*. When we allow fear to sneak in, we set ourselves up for brokenness. Remember, our goal is to return to the original intent that God has for us via restoration. Brokenness is also when we have something that is supposed to function as a whole, but has been interrupted. For example, my father recently broke his wrist. Unfortunately, because of the break it made it harder for him to do everyday common activities such as brushing his teeth, getting in and out of his truck, taking a shower and on and on. Our brokenness makes every day activities seem harder than they really are. As his wrist mended and the strength returned, he was able to go back to a normal life with a healthy wrist. He now has the knowledge of how important his wrist is, but most importantly, the condition of his wrist. He didn't realize the strength of his wrist, until he experienced the brokenness of it. We have been broken (interrupted) for so long that we don't really understand in how many ways the enemy has held us handicapped to our fears for many years.

Last, but certainly not least, we have to acknowledge our brokenness to God, take authority over our enemy, and allow God's resurrecting power to make us whole. Then and only then, can we experience the original position and condition that God created us to walk in.

May I lead you in a prayer?

Dear Heavenly Father,

I come to You in the name of Your precious Son and my personal Savior, Jesus Christ, and I ask You to forgive me for any way that I have judged myself according to my brokenness. Thank You Lord for teaching me that I don't have to live a day longer protecting my brokenness as if it is something that I deserve. I repent for operating in the fear of releasing my brokenness because the lack of knowledge convinced me that this was all life had to offer. I also repent for the way that I have judged others for breaking areas of my life that should have taught me love and kindness. I forgive my family members for teaching me their brokenness through any sort of abuse or misuse of my time and love. I also forgive anyone that has hurt me through means of rejection and abandonment. Please heal my brokenness and allow me to walk in this special place of wholeness. Lord teach me the principals of wholeness so that I may apply them to all the incomplete areas of my life. Guide me in the area of discernment, so that I can tell the difference in my brokenness from what I have called strength. Teach me how to create a nest where Your **GLORY** *can reside, and I can be at rest as You provide a way out for me. In Jesus' Name, Amen.*

<u>NOTES</u>

CHAPTER 6

WHAT IS TRUE INTIMACY?

True Intimacy is the missing piece of our puzzle called relationship! It is LOVE. It is the gift of life. It is the unconditional love that has become a stranger to life. It is the factor that determines the outcome of a process. The first example of this is recorded in Genesis, when God shared true intimacy in the garden with Adam and Eve. The garden atmosphere was the outcome of God's love. True intimacy was interrupted in the garden. Because of the fall of man, a counterfeit relationship took priority over the true intimacy that God offered man before his failure.

True intimacy has always been available, and it is effortless, but it does take obedient participation. Obedience is a major part of honor and respect that builds a platform for True Intimacy. True intimacy has been corrupted ever since the fall of man, but God wants to restore us to His original intentions of love and peace. We must know the difference between the counterfeit and the truth concerning love, and abide in that truth and love here on earth as it is in heaven. If we don't know true intimacy, then we can't have true intimacy. The Lord had to teach me what true intimacy was, because in my brokenness, I had settled with the counterfeit.

We have to make our minds up whether or not we will allow ourselves to be vulnerable to true intimacy as an elemental effect that will heal us, instead of steal from us. We are accustomed to operating under false intimacy to the point that we have lost our true identities. We have skeptically been impressed unconsciously, conceiving the idea of immorality of our society. True Intimacy has been available this whole time. Unfortunately, we have made vows with a false relationship out of comparison of our own failures. God bases His relationship with us on His love, not our inabilities to love or receive love. He is interested in our availabilities, more so than our abilities. I thought that the more that I could do for someone, the more they would love me. This is not true love! The Lord had to uncross the crossed wires in my brain concerning true love. True love (intimacy) lasts while false intimacy fades away. True intimacy heals while false intimacy steals. You have to know the difference in order to be set free. I had a lot of people in my life, but I didn't know how to truly love them.

The Word of God says that the reason we can love is because *"He first loved us" (1 John 4:19).* The *"enemy comes in like an angel of light" (2 Cor. 11:14)* to steal that love and replace it with the counterfeit, which is false intimacy. He is the counterfeit of the Light, so don't be surprised when something looks like God, only for you to find out that it is not God. The only difference in the word good and God is "O".

The closer that you get to My throne,
the more the enemy's voice sounds like My own.

The Word of God says that the sheep know the voice of the shepherd and no stranger will we follow. We have to discern the voice of God from the stranger's voice that convinces us that we are not loved. The Lord told me that, "The closer you get to My throne, the more the enemy's voice sounds like My Own." Here is where our discernment is supposed to kick in. Remember, discernment knows the difference between good and evil, and mature discernment is choosing good over evil. How many times have we thought that God told us something or maybe showed us something, and whatever the situation was, it never came to pass? This is the effect that our atmosphere has had on us because we were created for the love in the garden, but have dwelled in false intimacy in the wilderness. We were created for royalty, but somehow ended up in rags.

We have to be so careful because Satan knows our areas of brokenness. If we don't discern things, he can make us believe that things are going to work out one way and then when they don't, he will get us to blame God or even others. When God's will is coming to pass in our lives, there will always be evidence of peace and prosperity, not chaos and poverty. If we have places of poverty in our lives, we might want to discern this area and determine if God is the author of that poverty and confusion. As we discern this, we will have to choose the good (mature discernment).

"God is not the author of confusion" (1 Cor. 14:33). If there is confusion, it may be because God has torn down some self-made towers in your life. Just be real careful not to assume that He is at fault. The Tower of Babel in Genesis 11 was torn down by God because man was researching the stars, and astrology was being birthed. God became angry with the people because they were trying to build a tower for themselves and to make their names great, so the Lord destroyed their works. If things are being destroyed in our lives, then we need to seek the face of God to see the truth of "why" these things were built.

> And they said, Come, let us build us a city and a tower whose top reaches into the sky, and let us make a name for ourselves, lest we be scattered over the whole earth.
>
> Genesis 11:4, AMP

True Love Builds Up, Not Tears Down

We have built towers of false intimacy and called it love, but in all actuality, it hasn't been true love. True love (intimacy) heals and makes whole. True love is patient and kind, gentle and long suffering. As you choose the good and the truth sets you free, you realize that God is going before you and making a way. His mercy will tear down things that would stop or hinder His will from coming to pass in our lives. This is His mercy. We just have to line up with His plan. Maybe if things haven't worked out for us in the past, it was because we were abiding in our brokenness, instead of His wholeness. Try His way and see what happens! The plan that He has for us is a plan of true intimacy, and His love always prospers us.

> For I know the thoughts and plans that I have for you, says the Lord, thoughts and plans for welfare and peace and not for evil, to give you hope in your final outcome.

> Jeremiah 29:11, AMP

We, so many times, operate out of performance seeking validation from others and tend to forget that God loves us no matter what. We don't have to perform for Him; we just need to be available to Him for true intimacy.

When I was a little girl and my dad would come in late from his second job tending to his crops, he would be exhausted from the long hours of his day. He was not only providing a good living for his family, but also performing out of his brokenness, because that's what his dad had taught him to do. His father didn't teach him true intimacy, but created a sense of, "If you provide for your family, that's what love is."

Now don't get me wrong, we do have to provide for our families. The Bible says, *"If a man doesn't work, he doesn't eat."* My father worked all of the time and came in late because his father worked all of the time and came in late. This was my father's only validation from his father, so that was what he knew to do for his children. When my dad travels with me to give the Father's Blessing at our conferences, he tells the story that he doesn't ever remember getting a hug from his father or grandfather his whole life. If we work all of the time and don't stop to love, what has our work provided? His mother died when he was seven, so that created even more invalidation (because of abandonment) for this precious child. My father was a great provider, but his fears of not being able to provide drove him to a place of staying constantly busy. He was exhausted most of the time and missed out on a lot of our activities. Can we see how the enemy comes in as a light?

I thank God for the time that I did get to spend out on the farm with my dad. He taught me how to be a good provider for my family, besides the fact that I can tie a knot like a marine and back a truck up for a hundred miles. *All things work for the good of those who are called according to His purpose (Rom. 8:28).* I missed spending more time with my father as a child, but since the devil has been found out, our relationship has been restored seven times greater than the previous (Prov. 6:31).

We can't give what we don't have, and we can only receive what we are able to handle.

Once I heard a story about a female pregnant dog that was run over by a vehicle. Unfortunately, it broke her hips and she had to drag herself around with her front legs. Shortly after the healthy puppies were born, 3 out of the 5 puppies drug themselves around with their front legs like their mother, but their hind legs were not broken. We have to be real careful not to drag ourselves in front of others, because it also affects their lives. We as parents validate our children out of our wholeness, but we invalidate them out of our brokenness. We will be talking more about this later in the book.

Light (true intimacy) validates
Darkness (false intimacy) invalidates

Here are a few truths about true intimacy and what is available to us as we learn how to love. I hope that as you read these truths, it will help you to better understand what has been missing and how to receive it for yourselves. Can I lead you in a little prayer?

Dear God,

I repent for any way that I have allowed false intimacy to keep me from finding the true love that You have to offer me. Help me to understand TRUE INTIMACY so that I can share it with you and others. In Jesus' name, Amen.

Truths About True Intimacy

- The Glory of God cannot be touched by man, only experienced by true intimacy.
- True intimacy will always be understood by the ones who experience it, and it brings forth the fruits of the Spirit. If you have had a hard time producing the fruits of the Spirit, you may want to consider being available for true intimacy.
- If you misunderstand something, it is because of the lack of true intimacy.
- True intimacy is a master of communication.
- True intimacy is when you give all that you have, and you expect nothing in return.
- True intimacy doesn't expect you to fall; it picks you up when you do fall.
- True intimacy appears when you are able to look someone eye to eye and not be afraid.
- True intimacy heals places that have been broken for generations.
- True intimacy brings forth the glory of God that dissolves generational curses.
- True intimacy should be experienced by everyone, every day, as this was and is God's original intention.
- True intimacy is taught in the first 10 years of a child's life. They spend the rest of their lives choosing whether to operate under true or false intimacy. Time tells the difference between true and false intimacy.

- True intimacy lasts for all eternity. True intimacy will call forth pleasure, and as it comes forth, pain melts in its presence.
- True intimacy is a platform that the baby rests on when lying on its mother's breasts.
- God didn't call man and wife to be roommates. He called them to be true in-ti-mates. The lack of true intimacy will make you dread going home.
- True intimacy places a child within the womb of its mother.
- True intimacy places one woman's child in another woman's heart and home.
- True intimacy will always make sure others are satisfied, and that satisfies you.
- True intimacy allows you to find joy in someone else's victory.
- Fear will try to paralyze you from experiencing true intimacy. True intimacy makes others available for deliverance.
- When you have true intimacy with Jesus, you can never be satisfied with false intimacy. When you have true intimacy with Jesus, you are able to have true intimacy with everyone in your presence.
- True intimacy desires companionship.
- True intimacy desires to share all with all.
- True intimacy forgives.
- True intimacy flows and fulfills; false intimacy forces and leaves empty. If you don't have peace, it is because there is a lack of true intimacy. Seek true intimacy! Ask God to impregnate you with true intimacy.
- True intimacy operates by conception.
- True intimacy is when the truth penetrates and saturates you to the point that you are willing to trust. The lack of true intimacy will create trust issues deep within you that will grow roots of resentment and bitterness.
- True intimacy cannot be bought; it has to be sought.
- True intimacy always heals brokenness.

- True intimacy doesn't need help; it only needs an opportunity to heal.
- True intimacy doesn't take chances; it succeeds in everything that it attempts.
- True intimacy knows that it knows. The only way to get your brokenness fixed is true intimacy with the Father.
- True intimacy has to be a way of living in order to be made whole. The more healed you become, the more true intimacy you desire. After being made whole by way of true intimacy, you begin to operate in true intimacy at all times and all counterfeits must flee.
- True intimacy is a foundation for faith; false intimacy is a foundation for fear.
- True intimacy brings forth peace that surpasses all understandings.
- True intimacy fills you to the point of overflow. Overflow attracts the emptiness in others.
- True intimacy exposes us to the point of true deliverance, and it desires honesty.
- True intimacy operates in confirmation, not condemnation.
- True intimacy delivers.
- True intimacy convinces you that you deserve to be free.
- True intimacy is not afraid of trust.
- True intimacy will bring you out of your present day traumas.
- True intimacy believes in Him and in you.
- The day that you make the decision to get over yourself will be the introduction to true intimacy.
- True intimacy is when you can have peace with yourself.
- True intimacy isn't limited; it is fresh every morning.
- True intimacy is where revelation resides, and it always comes to teach you something. Humility will always introduce you to true intimacy.
- If you don't have true intimacy, you can't give true intimacy.

- True Intimacy is the pathway to our Destiny.
- True intimacy is a landing pad for God's glory.
- When knowledge and obedience get together, then wisdom can build a foundation for true intimacy.
- True intimacy bares all; nakedness brings humility.
- Because of the fall of man, perversion became known as relationship. However, perversion has to bow to true intimacy.
- True intimacy changes a person's countenance; you cannot have true intimacy without the company of joy and peace.
- True intimacy is not a feeling; it is a healing.
- True intimacy demands participation to be effective.
- True intimacy gives you authority.
- True intimacy is when you don't have time to mow your lawn, and your dad shows up unannounced and mows it for you.

True intimacy is like the SHALOM of God:

Nothing is missing; nothing is broken. If you can't love yourself, it is impossible to have true intimacy with others.

True Intimacy is being able to love yourself!

Lord, bring Your Kingdom of true intimacy down to earth as it is in heaven.

True Intimacy Births Validation

True intimacy brings forth validation. '*Validation*' is defined as "recognizing, establishing, or illustrating the worthiness or legitimacy of something or someone." True intimacy is the only avenue for validation. Our parents are a very vital part of validating us as children. If others fail to validate us, then our lives seemingly take the route of hardship, going over many bridges of troubled waters. Validation has to be experienced via true intimacy. The amount of validation that we receive as a child will be the evidence of our relationships in the future with other people and our children.

A father is chiefly in charge of validating a little girl's feministic characteristics. This is where we have to be careful, even in speaking over our unborn children about what gender child we desire. True intimacy accepts people for who they are, not what others desire them to be. We see an example of this in Luke 1 where Zacharias' mouth was muted to keep him from saying anything negative about the child that was in Elizabeth's womb. He was an older man at this point of the pregnancy. The older that we get in our brokenness, the more negative we become. Let's repent of our invalidations that have allowed our negativity, before it is too late. The reason we judge others so harshly is because we have not been validated, and we become jealous of other's validation.

Jealousy is the evidence of invalidations.
Jesus is the ultimate validation.

We must allow true intimacy to form validation within us and remove all residues from past invalidations that formed false foundations of intimacy. Remember, you can't give what you don't have, so therefore, if you have not been validated, you can't validate others. If you find yourself constantly walking away from people, it may not be them. This may be evidence of invalidation on your behalf. Too many times we tend to walk away from things in our lives that we can't overcome easily.

Invalidations make us **holey**. Validations make us **holy**. How do we become **whole**, when we have so many **holes**? Wholeness is a place that true intimacy desires to take you to in your life. It is a place that you have always dreamed of going, but couldn't ever quite make it to. It's like a vacation that you know you would enjoy, but you also have the reality of not having enough resources to get you there. The glory of God that is available for you to receive is like having unlimited frequent flyer miles accumulated for the rest of your life. Remember, the glory comes to take you from where you are to where you are going. Life in general should be a vacation, but instead vacations are usually visitations.

> And all of us, as with unveiled face, [because we] continue to behold [in the Word of God] as in a mirror the glory of the Lord, are constantly being transfigured into His very own image in ever increasing splendor and from one degree of glory to another; [for this comes] from the Lord [Who is] the Spirit.
>
> 2 Corinthians 3:18, AMP

The Word of God says, *"He is a Holy God, and that He must have a Holy people" (Lev. 11:45).* Holiness does not come by way of good works, as some denominations believe. This false doctrine will leave you in a state of emptiness and cause you to become bitter at God and at others. Example: When we begin to serve the Lord, we assume that the more we do, the more rewards we receive. In all actuality, all we receive is weariness, and the Bible warns us to *"not grow weary in doing good" (Gal. 6:9).* Have you ever said or had the thought that, "Nobody knows how much I do for others?" This is evidence of your invalidation, because if you were doing it in your wholeness instead of your brokenness, you would have had peace fill you. No one has to pat you on the back when you operate out of validations. Don't worry, my friend, if this explains the way that you have felt; just know that God wants to make you whole and fill in your holes. We become holy when we rest in God's love, and as we rest, we learn how to abide in His presence.

He wrote this to us because He knew that our brokenness would take us into a place of ritual and repetition instead of relationship. People expect so much out of each other that we automatically operate by what others expect out of us, instead of sanctification. Holiness comes by way of sanctification. The sanctification process consists of finding your brokenness (things that led you into captivity) and allowing His true intimacy to heal those places and set you free. When we justify our brokenness, we disqualify ourselves for holiness. Justification is evidence of weaknesses. Evidence of false intimacy would be expecting others and ourselves to eventually fail. False intimacy is the evidence of failures, and true intimacy is the evidence of overcoming obstacles. Obstacles are meant to interrupt intimacy!

Justification is the counterfeit to sanctification.

Holiness is the end result of wholeness, which comes by way of repentance. This brings forth restoration. As long as we justify our actions and reactions, we allow our brokenness to remain. Sanctification comes when we are made whole, and the next phase after being sanctified is to be glorified. Isn't this good news? We can be sanctified and glorified right here on earth as we will be in heaven. You may be thinking to yourself right now, "This woman has lost it!" Remember, kingdom is "whatever you lose, you always get back." You might want to try losing it for yourself, it's a lot better than thinking you have it, when you don't.

If you are full of holes (brokenness), then you are holey. This is satan's way: counterfeit holey living. If you allow God's love to heal (fill in) your holes (brokenness), as He heals you and you become whole, the next process of completion is HOLINESS. Therefore, the deeper you allow God to go into the most intimate places of your being that you have never allowed anyone to explore, His very presence will heal those places that you thought could never be healed (like the depths of the earth were filled when God's Spirit hovered over it). It was the process of filling the deep places of the earth with His Spirit that brought forth His light and His pleasure. When we allow God's Spirit to fill in the dark, deepest places of brokenness, it's then when He says, "This is good." This is when God is pleased.

Holes will keep you from holy.

The Word of God says, *"Be still and know that I am God"* *(Ps. 46:10)*. Brokenness calls for busyness. If we are busy trying to prove our holiness, then we might miss the opportunity that God has given us to be healed and become holy. When you are made whole, you don't have to prove this to anyone, it is for you. Again, we have to be careful not to be as the Pharisees when they were cleaning the outside of the cup while leaving the inside unclean. God wants you healed.

Can we just pray right now for the way that we have operated unconsciously under the deception of false intimacy and how it has kept us from our true destiny of true intimacy? True intimacy will cause you to be accurate, excellent and extraordinary.

Dear Heavenly Father,

We come to You now in the name of Jesus, Your only begotten Son, and our precious Savior, and ask for Your forgiveness concerning our participation in all activities of false intimacy. We repent of how false intimacy has left us feeling as if we had to perform for Your love. We allow You to fill the broken areas of our lives that have left so many holes that we felt like a void. We repent of any and all fears that we have had causing us to think that we had to be a certain way before You would love us and accept us. We also repent for the rejection that we have operated under concerning our relationship with You, in comparison to our earthly parents and grandparents. We forgive our earthly parents and grandparents for any way that they introduced us to false intimacy. We know, Lord, that they did the best that they could. We also repent for justifying our unhealthy emotions and prolonging unnecessary sufferings and calling this a relationship with You. Please forgive us, Father, as we forgive ourselves. We repent for any and all abandonment issues involved as a result of false intimacy, and we cancel the devil's assignment now, in Jesus' Name. Lord, please show me the areas in my life that I have justified because I didn't know how to be set free. Please forgive me for any way that I have justified myself and/or others as a means of self protection or defense. Holy Spirit, please show me Your truth about true intimacy.

NOTES

CHAPTER 7

WHAT IS FALSE INTIMACY?

Anything that leaves you empty and void. False Intimacy breeds misunderstanding, chaos, confusion, division, retaliation, divorce, destruction, and devastation, which are all precursors to the death of a relationship. This is a foundation of deception that has been created by satan to dilute the power of relationship. We were created for relationship. Satan knew that if he could interrupt the natural way of living, he would create an unnatural connection between people. There would be no peace available because peace can only compliment truth. If peace is not forthcoming, then there apparently is an obvious lack of intimacy or a false foundation of intimacy. The lack of intimacy is just as bad as false intimacy. An example of this would be a woman allowing a man to abuse her (false intimacy) rather than being alone (lack of intimacy). This is what I call *"something better than nothing" mentality.* False Intimacy is the opposite of LOVE.

Be really careful not to assume that the other person is at fault. Take authority over your own level of brokenness, and seek healing for the relationship. After a period of seeking God for truth, He will direct your steps as you are made whole. Remember to lean not unto thine own understanding. How many relationships have we aborted because we refuse to deal with our heart's issues? Proverbs says, *"Out of the heart, the issues of life flow."* People will treat you how ever you allow them to. When we allow people to treat us unkind, it is because we have treated ourselves unkindly out of a relationship of false intimacy. When you receive true intimacy from the Father, you begin to practice that method with others, because it brings so much peace and joy.

> Keep thy heart with all diligence; for out it are the issues of life.
>
> Proverbs 4:23, KJV

In my brokenness, I would help others to keep myself occupied from not being able to help myself. In others words, it was easier to help others than to deal with my own stuff. This was validation to me from an unhealthy viewpoint. In my broken state, I would put up with a lot of unnecessary things and then later complain about it. Note: You don't have the right to complain about the things you tolerate! Nevertheless, when I was made whole by the power of the glory of God, things had to change. Once the glory of God sets you free, you no longer tolerate how people usually treat you. When you change, then other things have to change.

There was a lady who rented my house once and started threatening me that she was going to move out if I didn't do exactly what she told me to do, and I simply said, *"You've got to:"* She said, *"Excuse me?"* I said, *"You've got to."* And she said, *"I have to do what?"* *"Move out! Now!!!!"* She then began to apologize for the way she had talked to me and begged for me to let her stay. By this time I was healed and she no longer had the authority to speak to me unkindly. It shocked a lot of people when the Lord made me whole, because I no longer tolerated the way that they treated me.

When you are made whole, you don't tolerate brokenness.

Normally, if our hearts are full of brokenness, we either fall prey to people speaking to us any 'ole way, or we become so defensive that we hurt others before they get a chance to hurt us. The Word of God also says, *"Out of the abundance of the heart, the mouth speaketh"* *(Matt.*

114

12:34b). It is because of the issues of our hearts that we can't love our neighbors. If you are not experiencing true intimacy with your neighbor, then there is no way you can have it with your Father in heaven. We reproduce what is in our hearts. False intimacy would allow you to disconnect from people emotionally and place a wall between the two of you just to get you by. This is not relationship! False intimacy will lead you down the dark alley called Lonely Avenue! Rituals, traditions and routines will escort you to the place of desertion also known as false intimacy.

False Intimacy Tears Down

False intimacy produces invalidation. '*Invalidation*' (Webster's definition) means "to weaken or destroy the cogency or the ability to conceive or think." The ways of invalidation will encourage you to take care of yourself because nobody else will. This will cause an interruption in the way that you love others or receive love. It will also create an attitude within you that everybody is always after something that you possess. False intimacy is the proud father of twins, fear and failure. It also invites you to be available to the identity thief and creates a sense of failure deep within that only true love can heal. Invalidation allows generational curses to remain active in our lives and empowers the curse to affect our children. What we don't deal with in our lives today, will deal with our children's lives tomorrow. False Intimacy rejects any form of corrective criticism and claims it as judgment. When you are healed and made whole, corrective criticism will catapult you into your destiny. Corrective criticism, when based in love, will enable you to take the short cut to success.

When I take in children, I normally teach each one of them how to cook. One of my daughters was in this process of learning how to cook, but she would get her feelings hurt if I corrected her about her efforts. I would always praise her before I would correct her just to let her know how good she had done (although good is the enemy to best). In whatever endeavor my children undertake, I want them to give their best! However, her feelings would get hurt every time that I would correct her. She would automatically go into an apologetic mode and repeatedly say how sorry she was. Then she would disconnect from me, and go into another room and cry. She always knew that I would come right behind her, questioning her meltdown. The only way to get to the bottom of something that is buried deep within one's soul is to hit it head on and expose the issue that continuously tries to destroy us.

Neglecting deliverance will keep you under the rug of deception.

We would face the facts of her inefficiencies and determine what ingredients were needed to continue the cooking lessons. It took years of seeking to finally determine the outcome. It all boiled down to the fact that her mother did not validate her as a little girl in the kitchen, so therefore, several issues were at hand. My daughter had a weight problem because her birth mother allowed her to eat junk food a good majority of her life (this explained going off to another room and hiding). They were on food stamps, and my experience with this is that people who buy groceries with food stamps tend to go for the more convenient foods (such as junk). So therefore, cooking was obsolete and avoided, which explains the child not knowing how to cook. My daughter was not validated in this area, so she would become defensive about her lack of knowledge (pride). I've learned that the places that I usually defend about myself is evidence of my invalidation. She then felt as if she had failed, which flooded her emotions with a sense of unworthiness. This is also the evidence of invalidation. If a feeling of unworthiness is constantly trying to overwhelm you, this is the outcome of invalidations.

With time and patience, I was finally able to explain the pattern of invalidation to her. My teaching (love) validated her, which healed her and made her whole. The very thing that she learned, she could share and now help others in return. Since this validation, she has recently lost over one hundred pounds and has become a great cook! I really encourage you

116

to evaluate your unhealthy emotions as a sign to find your freedom from false intimacy.

Validation always brings deliverance!

In order to break generational curses in our lives, we must be willing to take the chance of allowing God to heal us and make us whole. Only then can we pass on a blessing of wholeness to our children, rather than passing on a generational curse. False intimacy allows generational curses to remain. We must take action and cancel this debt and provide a true inheritance to flow through us and on to the next generation. A true inheritance consists of leaving a legacy of validations for your children and grandchildren. We will be discussing generational curses in the next chapter.

**Remember, what we don't deal with in our lives
today, will deal with our children's lives tomorrow!**

False Intimacy Offers No Explanation

Invalidations introduce abandonment. A '*curse of abandonment*' over a child is created when a parent doesn't have a true intimate relationship with their child. This curse of abandonment consists of no commitment or communication from the parent or parents. This curse, if not broken and the parents forgiven, will interrupt your relationship with your Heavenly Father, as it does with others as well. This curse also has the power to impress the **'*curse of prostitution*',** as it comes to weaken relations and cause ruin in your line of generations. Abandonment drives the spirit of prostitution. A '*prostitute*' is "a person (as a writer or painter) who deliberately '*debases*' (to lower in status, esteem, quality, or character) his or her talents," according to Webster's dictionary. We assume that a prostitute always operates in a sexual misconduct, and this is one description that we know to be true. A prostitute operates in invalidations due to the lack of true intimacy. We fall short of wisdom when we judge what we assume may be wrong with ourselves and others.

You may be a prostitute and not know" it!

If you have ever debased yourself and/or your talents, which is rooted in self-bitterness, you have opened the door to spiritual prostitution. Spiritual prostitution prevents you from becoming a True Bride. The father is normally the one who escorts a bride to the altar. If and when this process is interrupted, there will be an identity crisis at the altar of your rightful Kingdom position. The father's original intention is to escort the bride (His daughter) to the place at the altar of covenant of true identity via true intimacy.

A father validates a little girl's femininity. Countless times, I have counseled women who despised their father's failed endeavors, only to marry a man of the same mortal make-up, trying to find acceptance one way or another. This altar is also where the father acts as a mentor and/or best man to a son in order that the son has knowledge of how to love the bride (the church). When interrupted, the enemy distorts this image to the point that the son puts more emphasis on a canine becoming his best friend because of the absence of his father's knowledge. Therefore, relationships "go to the dogs." If your natural father fails in this area, this will cause you to misinterpret courtship.

Courtship determines engagement, and engagement determines eternal outcomes.

The truth is we have all fallen short of God's glory (Romans 3:23). Because of invalidations and false intimacy, we fail to realize that we are His creation. We are *"fearfully and wonderfully made" (Ps. 139:14)*. We were not made to be full of fear and wonder why we were made! This spirit is the counterfeit in which we fall prey to, as we are in our bridal process of becoming whole. The opposite of a true bride is a prostitute. A prostitute becomes numb to her emotions, hates herself, and is bitter towards others. Prostitutes come in both male and female form. We must

118

learn *how* to be a bride in order to *be* a bride. Why settle with a lifetime of no relationship or continuous failures in relationships? Sound like anyone you know?

The point here that I'm trying to make is not to think of someone else that may suffer with these issues; my question is, "Do you?" If you can't love yourself, then this is evidence of prostitution. We have to love ourselves in order that we may love others. If not, we may eventually become enslaved to sexual sins.

Let me explain this a little more. If a woman can't receive her husband's love because of her invalidation issues, does it mean that her husband doesn't love her or does it mean that she can't receive his love? So many times we look for love in all the wrong places, only to find out eventually, it is our hearts that need mending instead of another adulterous relationship. If a husband has a hard time with commitment to his wife, is it his wife's fault or the fact that no relationship with his father (commitment, invalidation) has taken control over his morality? The root issue would be the lack of true intimacy from his father creating an illusion for this man to devalue himself, because he couldn't receive the commitment from his wife. In all actuality, he could not give commitment back to her and felt unworthy, so therefore, an extramarital affair was fulfilling.

Remember, unworthiness comes as evidence of invalidation.

We must get to the root issue in order to be released from the lie of our brokenness. Do we often wonder why our children go off on a tangent in their young lives seeking validation from others? It may be that we don't need to judge them because the root issue may be of our own doings. We must validate our children, or else they will seek other avenues of affection.

I know a couple who adopted two children, and because they were not attentive to their abandonment issues, their lives became miserable

119

because of their children's behaviors. Their son died at a very young age of HIV, and their daughter was promiscuous and eventually abandoned her three children. A lot of people assumed that, "they just got bad children." This is insane. Children don't come into this world bad! We have to take responsibility for our own issues, and a child will always come back to the truth that he has been taught.

> Train up a child in the way he should go [and in keeping with his individual gift or bent], and when he is old he will not depart from it.

> Proverbs 22:6, AMP

The truth is that if the adoptive parents would have broken the curse of abandonment (which comes from false intimacy) over these children, their lives would have been a lot different. We must seek the Lord to find the spiritual issues that are enabling such occurrences. Usually if our children aren't happy, it is because of invalidations that need to be healed.

Invalidations can be healed. Invalidations are a form of deception that the enemy uses against God's people to build false intimacy between parents and children, grandparents and grandchildren, husbands and wives. We cannot afford to continue to sweep such as this under rugs. We know throughout our lives the things that people do and say to us, make us or break us as individuals. When your mom tells you how smart you are and encourages you to excel, the chances of you being a successful adult (validation) are greater than that of her not telling you (invalidation).

An example of invalidation would be the mom calling the child stupid, lazy, no good, or saying things like, "You are just like your father, you will never amount to anything!" The chances of this young child becoming a successful adult are very slim. It is possible to be validated through other people besides your parents, but ultimately, it is the parents role to pursue validation within their children and even into their grandchildren. Everyone desires hearing something good about themselves. Validations heal and fill the emptiness that invalidation's bring.

Invalidation's are the effects birthed from generational curses.

Invalidation Leaves One Empty

One time I pulled up to a gas station to fill up my car and the tenant said, *"I'm sorry lady, but we don't have any gas today."* I thought to myself, "this looks like a gas station. There are gas pumps to prove this. The tenant looks like a gas pumper, but he has no gas to pump. Is this a figment of my imagination, or do I really need gas? If you think that it is a gas station because it looks like one, but if it doesn't have gas, is it really a gas station?" Just because it didn't have gas, didn't change the fact that I was on empty and needed fuel. A lot of times when our needs aren't met by others (our parents or grandparents), it doesn't mean that we don't still have a need!

Every child has emotional needs and has to be validated in order for these needs to get met physically, spiritually, emotionally, and mentally. Sometimes our parents (grandparents) look like parents, but if they don't have validation themselves, they can look like parents all day, and your emotional needs as a child still go empty. Let's take another look at the definition of the word '*validate*,' which according to Webster's, says "to recognize, establish, or illustrate the worthiness or legitimacy of." '*Validation*' means "an act, process, or instance of validating." '*Valid*' means "strong, potent: well rounded."

To illustrate this point, a dog trainer will train any dog, no matter the breed of the animal or whether it came from the best or the worst of bloodlines. Remember, we are all adopted.

Validation illustrates identity.

121

For [the spirit which] you have now received [is] not a spirit of slavery to put you once more in bondage to fear, but you have received the Spirit of adoption [the Spirit producing sonship] in [the bliss of] which we cry, Abba (Father!) Father!"

Rom. 8:15, AMP

Validations cure relationship identity insecurities. Some of the best dogs that I have had in the past were what people generally call strays. If the trainer treats the dog with respect, caring for its needs, and rewarding it when it obeys, this animal becomes validated by his trainer. Validation brings obedience. If your children are disobedient, consider validating them and see what happens. Obedience brings blessings (Deut. 28).

Validation Brings Obedience, and Obedience Brings Blessings

You might say, "Now wait a minute! Are you comparing me to a dog?" It's better than me comparing you to a donkey! Where did this situation go south? If your parents did not or are not validating you, it is probably because they have not been validated themselves. They look like a gas tenant, but they are out of gas! Remember, you can't give what you don't have. If you have never trained a dog, you cannot call yourself a dog trainer. If you don't have gas, you cannot call yourself a gas station. If you are not validated by your parents, then chances of you validating your children are as great as a gas tenant training dogs!!!

We have to go back to the first and revisit our own training. How were you validated as a child? Did your mother instill qualities in you to call forth excellence, or did she in her self-pity make you wonder if things could ever be possible? Did your father validate you in ways that strengthened your inner man, or did he constantly put you down and weaken, or maybe even destroy you, on the inside? I have the BEST parents in this world, but remember they couldn't give what they didn't have. We are not trying to beat up on Mom and Dad here. We are just going a little deeper, and becoming more excellent sons and daughters of God, and in return that makes us better moms and dads for our children and grandchildren.

If you're reading these words, and you are becoming a bit uncomfortable about your childhood and/or the way you have treated your children, I encourage you to keep reading. You've already bought the book; you might as well go ahead and get your money's worth. The truth hurts, but it sets you free (John 8:32). You will know the truth and the truth will set you free.

We are not accountable for what we don't know. Invalidation is the evidence of generational curses and validation is the evidence of generational blessings. We are only accountable for what we do know. Hosea 4:6 says, *"My people are destroyed for the lack of knowledge. Because you, the priestly nation, have rejected knowledge, I will also reject you that you shall be no priest to me. Seeing you have forgotten the law of your God, I will also forget your children."* Let's know why things are like they are for us and if they are not working out for us and our children, let's seek God's truth, and let Him set us free. **Hallelujah**. Let's come into the fullness of being made whole as a child and/or a parent at this point. Let's get set free.

Here are a few ways you can try validating your children and grandchildren. It's not too late to start now!

Validations void and cancel all invalidations.

Here are a few validations that may help you get started:

35/17   I'm so proud of you, son/daughter, for doing well at school.

35/17   I knew that you could do it.

35/17   I appreciate all that you do and have done for me.

35/17   I couldn't have made it without your help.

35/17   I'm so proud of you.

$\frac{35}{17}$ Great job!

$\frac{35}{17}$ I am so blessed to have you as a son/daughter.

$\frac{35}{17}$ I'm proud of the decisions that you have made.

$\frac{35}{17}$ There is greatness in you.

$\frac{35}{17}$ You can do all things.

$\frac{35}{17}$ You can be anything that you desire to be.

$\frac{35}{17}$ You are successful and will continue to walk in success.

$\frac{35}{17}$ You are so beautiful or handsome.

Let's get set free from invalidations ourselves so we can validate others, and overcome any and all generational curses on us and our loved ones in Jesus' name.

We make associations with our past pains and failed relationships to the point that we hold things against the one true Father. We must get to the point in our lives that we first realize that our invalidations led us to our brokenness, and our brokenness has left us empty and confused as to what relationship is truly about. It is love that is going to set us free! Tina Turner sings a song about "What's love got to do with it?" In all actuality, it has everything to do with it! If you don't have love, you don't have God (1 John 4:8).

We need to learn how to love to be able to
fight the wiles of our enemy.

If God's way is all loving, then the opposite of this must be unloving. This unloving spirit will keep you from loving others and disable you from receiving love. Love is what heals. When we have hate (an act of not loving) in our hearts it's because of the level of unforgiveness that we are operating under. If we are under unforgiveness, then this means that we are in bondage to it, as it is over us. There needs to be a change of position, because what we are under takes authority over us. We must forgive and get over this sin of holding onto the wrongs that have besieged us for generations. The Word of God says that we must *"forgive in order to be forgiven" (Matthew 6:14).* If we have a pain associated with a past memory, then there is a fountain of unforgiveness springing up out of our heart. You may say, "Well I forgive so and so for what they did, but I will never forget it." This is not forgiveness. The pain that you still hold onto in your heart needs to be healed, and as long as you allow it to stay, it will hurt you and others.

Remember, HURT PEOPLE, HURT PEOPLE.

If you want to be an instrument used in God's orchestration, we need to make ourselves available for His love to mend our broken strings.

Again, the only truth behind false intimacy is building a relationship on a foundation of fear, pillars of mistrust, walls of deception, and a covering of insecurities. False Foundations will always fall. Remember the story of the "Three Little Pigs and the Big Bad Wolf." Or better yet, do you remember the story in Matthew 7:24-27? Remember, don't point your finger at others because there will be three pointing back at you. Let's quit blaming others and make ourselves available for a healing.

Truths About False Intimacy

- False intimacy has no life; it eventually fades away.
- False intimacy is afraid to laugh.
- False intimacy always brings confusion.
- If you are in a relationship of false intimacy, the confusion will keep you out of the greater glory, and you will have mere conversation.
- False intimacy will always encourage hesitation, procrastination and devastation.
- False intimacy is escorted by accusations.
- Lack of communication will promote false intimacy.

125

- False intimacy is the evidence of the loss of power. Remember when you first accepted the Lord, and how powerful you were in your relationship with Him? Over a period of time you lost your zeal and became stagnant. This is participation in false intimacy!
- False intimacy consists of rituals, traditions, and routines.
- Misery is an emotion that stems from false intimacy.
- Intimidation introduces false intimacy.
- If we can't enjoy ourselves, this is evidence of false intimacy. We are the apple of His eye!
- We cover ourselves up with false intimacy and we call it God.
- Fear is founded in false intimacy.
- False intimacy pushes the pride in us to the point that we think that we are always right and everyone else is wrong.
- Condemnation is built from false intimacy.
- We obligate ourselves out of false intimacy and call this "good deeds."
- When you base your relationship on false intimacy, it always leaves you empty.
- False intimacy interrupts wisdom. The lack of knowledge is bred from false intimacy, and it always destroys God's children.
- The Pharisees and Sadducees operated in false intimacy when they acted as if they had it together, but really had no relationship with anyone.
- False intimacy will encourage you to blame others for things that you think that you have lost that really never belonged to you.
- False intimacy is sin.
- The difference between false intimacy and true intimacy is that with false intimacy, you have nothing in common. With true intimacy, you get in a rhythmical procession of continuous complete communication.
- False intimacy forces and true intimacy flows.
- False intimacy requires forgiveness.
- When you visit places of false intimacy, the process will take longer, and you will feel as if you have been raped.

- Trying to be something you're not is a form of false intimacy.
- False intimacy is trying to give something you don't have.
- False intimacy will make you try to prove yourself.
- False intimacy convinces you that freedom has deserted you.
- False intimacy always puts you in competition with others.
- False intimacy refuses to say, "I'm sorry." It makes excuses instead of apologies.
- False intimacy is the action that enslaves you to sin.

May we pray?

Dear Father in Heaven,

Thank You so much for loving me the way that You do. I repent for any way that I have not appreciated Your love for me or any way that I have ever taken Your love for granted. I also repent for any way that I have abused the love that You have given to me as an example of how to love myself and others. Thank You for being a perfect example for me to follow. I forgive myself for any way that I have abused myself in this area of love and release myself to receive the fullness of Your love, Father. In Jesus' Name, I forgive everyone that has ever let me down in the area of loving me or rejecting my love as a gift that would bring healing instead of division. I cancel any and all debts of false intimacy and any and all involvement in any relationship of false intimacy that tried to deceive me and make me think that this was true love. I also break and shatter any unhealthy soul ties that I may have made with others out of a false intimate relationship. I ask that You forgive me for the way that I have allowed my invalidations to unrighteously judge the way that You love me. Set me free from any areas of invalidations that are operating in my life, and validate me wholly. Again, Father, I thank You for showing Your ultimate love towards me by sending Your only begotten Son to die for me on that cross. Please help me to know love, and as I know this truth, may it set me totally free, in Jesus' Name.

NOTES

CHAPTER 8

PERSONALITIES OF GENERATIONAL CURSES

What is a generational curse? A generational curse is a curse on your life that your ancestors allowed to become part of your life. It is a repetitious pattern of destruction that follows you and your family throughout the ends of time. Its goal is to destroy you and your loved ones prematurely and has traumatic intentions. The revelation of God **unveils the hidden mysteries of generational curses** that will lead you to break these curses for yourself and the welfare of your family. A lot of people don't want to admit that generational curses exist. I've actually had people to argue with me about generational curses, because they didn't want to admit that it may be a possibility. Many times the things that frustrate us may be because we don't have the answers to these questions. That's when we must seek to find.

I assure you that God is in control and will meet you where you are at and deliver you according to your heart's desire to become free. Maybe it is the lack of teaching on the subject matter, or possibly the lack of responsibility required after receiving knowledge of this matter. Whatever the case, generational curses that are ignored are the ones that are empowered. If you hang your clothes out on the line to dry with the knowledge of a storm coming, it's your fault if they get wet.

According to the Webster's dictionary, *'revelation'* is "the act of revealing or communicating divine truth: something that is revealed by God to humans: an act of revealing to view or making known." There are things in our lives that we know because of what others teach us. Past experiences also leave impressions on us. The things that God reveals to us are things that are truths that separate us from what others have taught us wrong, regardless of good intentions. Whatever the case may be, it is the revelation of God that separates us from things that have the ability to destroy us (which is the lack of knowledge).

So many times, we fall in areas of our lives that require the seeking of the truth of God to set us free from things we know that are coming to steal, kill, and destroy. It is up to us to seek out the hidden mysteries of the past generations and ask God to give us the key to unlock the doors of prosperity that have been locked down for generations past. The key is the revelation of God! God not only has a doorway of opportunities for us to walk through, He also has a hallway of inheritance waiting for us to explore.

The Lord told me at the well that day that everything that my ancestors could not receive, He would give to me because of my obedience. As the Lord revealed things to me about my past generations, I drew nigh to Him, and He met me and took me into a place of freedom. Since the writing of this book, I have witnessed many generational curses broken by the blood of Jesus Christ.

I thought my whole life that the things that I went through were because of how I was. In fact, it wasn't how I was as much as it was the *"personality"* of the generational curse that I was under. It manifests as a personality because of the reality of it being a spirit; spirits do not show ownership. They operate out of a domineering demise. They have to have permission to reside, and they can be evicted at any time. They cannot be faithful to the curse, because darkness is not faithful to anyone or anything. So therefore, it can only manifest through places within a person that are already broken. Brokenness is darkness! Darkness cannot comprehend light; it can only compliment darkness.

I thought my whole life that the things that I went through were because of how I was.

And the Light shines on in the darkness, for the darkness has never overpowered it [put it out or absorbed it or appropriated it, and is unreceptive to it].

John 1:5, AMP

For an example, the only way that a generational curse of poverty can operate in your life is for your existing brokenness to compliment the curse. Existing brokenness could be greed, unjust gain, covetousness, not tithing your money to God or gambling, just to name a few that relate to the curse of poverty. If there is a pattern of poverty traced in the last four generations, you will want to repent for the love of money (I Tim. 6:10), and forgive the people in your life that should have validated you in the Wisdom of financial prosperity. As you seek the Father for healing, He will take you into a place that not only sets you free from the perversions of finances, but it will also seal up the holes where the finances seep through.

Now therefore thus says the Lord of hosts, Consider your ways and set your mind on what has come to you. You have sown much, but you have reaped little; you eat, but you do not have enough; you drink, but you do not have your fill; you clothe yourselves, but no one is warm; and he who earns wages has earned them to put them in a bag with holes in it. Thus says the Lord of hosts: Consider your ways, (your previous and present conduct) and how have you fared.

Haggai 1:5-7, AMP

Consider,' according to Webster's dictionary, is defined as, "to gaze on steadily or reflectively." We must reflect upon our last four generations and study any patterns of disruption in order to be set free from any curse that tries to take dominion over our lives.

To gaze steadily or reflectively.

We Are To Analyze Our Past, Not Sympathize With Our Past

When we sympathize with our past, we turn into a pillar of salt (Gen. 19:26). Sympathy brings self-pity! When we analyze our past, we become the salt of the earth (Matt. 5:13). This scripture goes on to say in the Amplified Bible, "If the salt loses its taste (its strength, its quality), how can its saltiness be restored? It is not good for anything any longer but to be thrown out and trodden underfoot by men." If you feel "troddened" by other people, then maybe you need to consider analyzing your past, instead of being sympathetic concerning your past. Walk away and don't look back, your past cannot enter into your DESTINY!

I have heard my whole life that there are two kinds of people: the have's and the have not's! This is a lie and the curse needs to be broken. This is what the Word of God has to say about it:

> For God shows no partiality [undue favor or unfairness; with
> Him one man is not different from another].

> Romans 2:11, AMP

Generational Curses conceal themselves to the point that they want you to believe that God does for one and not the other. I truly believe that if God did it for Moses, He will also do it for me! Is this too much of the truth to believe? When I was under a financial generational curse, I couldn't understand why I worked so hard but never had anything. I thought of myself as a "have not." When the curse was broken, I could finally see what God had intended for me. I then realized that it was the personality of the curse that told me that I was less than what I could be.

If you think of yourself less than what God intended for you, then you may want to consider your ways and set your mind on the things that have come to you. *"As a man thinketh in his heart, so is he" (Proverbs 23:7)*. We just repent right now in Jesus' Name of the ways that we thought that God would do for others and would not do for us.

132

I ministered to a lady not long ago who was under a curse of poverty, and the Lord set her and her husband free. The judgment that allowed the curse to remain active was that of which was against her father. He gambled his paycheck away every Friday, causing his wife and children to live in poverty. She never forgave her father, and as a result, the curse came upon her (unforgiveness will hold you to a curse of poverty). She and her husband constantly fought about finances (even paying tithes), but after repenting for judgment and unforgiveness towards her father, the glory of God renewed her.

Now her husband supports her efforts towards the ministry (and has even paid his tithes) and they no longer argue about finances. He doesn't attend church with her, but he now sends his blessings with her. They used to live from paycheck to paycheck, but now they have money left over to enjoy. She was taking out her frustrations on her husband, blaming him for the mistakes that her father made, but it was her heart's issues that needed to be addressed. Remember, our frustrations usually come because we don't have the answers to certain questions.

Repentance always brings forth renewal!

An example of breaking a generational curse of abandonment would be if you were given away as a child and grow up to have children, a sure way to break this curse would be to come out of agreement with abandonment. Decree and declare that not another one of your generational offspring will be displaced, and raise your own children successfully. Just because a curse decided to fall upon you because of others' iniquities, it doesn't mean that you have to put up with it. Break it and be free. After all, a family reunion isn't a lot of fun with just a few people! If we would be obedient in this area of deliverance of abandonment, the Department of Family and Children Services would have to draw unemployment!

My mother was given away as a child and my father's mother died when he was seven. They too could have decided to operate under a generational curse of abandonment, but instead chose to break the curse. Because of their obedience of raising their own children, between me and my sister we have now taken in over twenty-five kids. Be ready when you break a curse for the blessings of the Lord to flood and overtake you for generations to come.

My grandfather squandered a good part of my inheritance, and as I reflected and studied this pattern of destruction, I was able to break a generational curse. Now my inheritance is being returned to me at this present time. As the manifestation of generational curses take place, they come as a personality to fool us into thinking that it is of our own, only to line up with the power of darkness that is allowed by our brokenness.

It was only when I repented for the lackadaisical level of acknowledgment concerning my own finances, and actually forgave my grandfather for his uncanny cares about his, that I began to see a difference financially. Fear, rejection, and abandonment issues allow a legal access which brings forth the evidence of generational curses. In other words, there is no truth to it; truth is the only thing that shows possession. A generational curse can only possess you if you give it permission to. You can't possess something that you don't own; this is a lie. Satan has domain on this earth, but he does NOT hold the deed.

There Is No Substance To A Lie, Only Personality

The lie in this instance was the accusatory rumors that I received from others toward my grandfather who died when I was three. Better yet, it was judgment that I had placed on my grandfather from what I had heard from other people. Remember, false intimacy will tell you that you've lost something in the past that didn't belong to you, just to get you to judge another. I really didn't know my grandfather, yet I had judged him all my life from what others had told me about his lifestyle. Their accusations were birthed out of their jealousies. The personality of the generational curse that was on his life could remain active in my life only if I judged him. *"Judge not, lest ye shall be judged with the same measure" (Matt. 7:1).*

'*Personality*' is defined by Webster's as "the totality of an individual's behavioral and emotional characteristics." We have to realize that a personality is formed out of experiences due to good or bad impressions and how these affect us as human beings. So it is only when we have brokenness that a generational curse can express itself through us to bring more damage than to the previous person that it attacked.

A generational curse always has to manifest itself as broken in the same manner as it comes to destroy.

The next day after I broke this curse, my mother testified to me that my father spoke of his father's goodness for the first time in forty-five years (she had no idea that I had broken the curse). My father had never said anything bad about his father, but he had never mentioned his father's goodness either. In the natural, my father was affected by the curse being broken and began to testify how good his father was. The curse that I broke just the day before released my father to speak of the goodness of his father. The Word of God says that when we obey the voice of God, He blesses us for a thousand generations (Deut. 5:10). This doesn't only apply to our children, it can also apply up the lineage to our parents and grandparents, even our aunts, uncles, and cousins. **Hallelujah!**

A personal experience that exposed another generational curse in my life was one of a traumatic ordeal that happened when I was nine. It left me devastated and confused about the ingredients of a healthy relationship. Confusion permits errors. Have you ever wondered why error has been a major part of your past experiences (some call it mistakes)? Confusion always permits error! The confusion that brings forth errors may be a personality of a generational curse that needs to be broken. This confusion took me down many roads of relational disasters that kept me from finding true intimacy. This was not of my own doings!

135

It was the enemy's plan to keep me from finding true intimacy. Many times we confusingly associate our natural experiences with our supernatural abilities to be loved. This disables us from true intimacy! True intimacy (love) from our Heavenly Father is the only thing that will heal us and set us free.

Generational curses will appear suddenly, but they could take years to figure out because of our allowance of fear. As long as we operate in fear, discernment can't take its rightful position. Fear will also keep you in a place of lack of knowledge, and we know from Hosea 4:6 that this will destroy God's children. When we realize that this is not of our own doings, but that of a personality of a generational curse, it's only then that we can come out from under all of the guilt and shame, and pin the curse down with rightful blame. When we become free of the guilt and shame, allow discernment to do its job and cancel the curse, the glory of God then can make us WHOLE.

Generational Curses are Destiny Robbers

Just like any other child, I dreamed of what I would become one day. I would imagine myself in the finest courtrooms around the world defending people who had been victimized. I daydreamed often of the offender being dragged away to his final destination of divine justice (I've always rooted for the underdog). My life suddenly took a turn toward days of depression when the generational curse of my ancestors arose to defeat my purpose and plans of plaintiveness. The devil thought if he could knock me out first, then I wouldn't have a shot at him. What he forgot was that I am a child of The Most High God of Israel, and I don't have to fight my battles. My battles have already been fought and won. *"He said, Hearken, all Judah, you inhabitants of Jerusalem, and you King Jehoshaphat. The Lord says this to you: Be not afraid or dismayed at this great multitude; for the battle is not yours, but God's."* (2 Chron. 20:15 AMP)

This battle is not yours.

This satanic impression held me captive for thirty years until the glory of God arose and healed me of my affliction. Traumas are manifestations of Generational Curses. It wasn't me as much as it was the personality of the generational curse!

> But unto you who revere and worshipfully fear My name shall the Sun of Righteousness arise with healing in His wings and His beams, and you shall go forth and gambol like calves [released] from the stall and leap for joy.
>
> Malachi 4:2, AMP

Court and confusion was then dismissed. The great thing about breaking generational curses is that they may operate for centuries before they are figured out, and they may get away with a lot of devastation that God is blamed for. In the end, when they are found out, everything has to be returned to the rightful owner. In other words, the trauma that I underwent will never come upon my children, my children's children, or my great-grandchildren. **Hallelujah**! When we break generational curses, that puts our children in the next position of blessings!

This curse attacked my intelligence to the point that I could not study, complete my work, or excel in honorable activities. I was never an "A" average kid. My average was a sixty-nine point nine, because I knew that was what would get me by. So many times as Christians, we simply do what gets us by, but it may be due to the effects of a generational curse. God doesn't want us to just get by, He wants us to excel and prevail.

My sister and I attended a Baptist College together. She was on the Dean's list, and I was on his prayer list. I could never pull it together because I was stuck in my trauma. This curse interrupted the way that I would conceive information. Remember, conception of truth introduces you to completion when offered by true intimacy. Conception of deception brings forth incompletion by way of false intimacy. I would hear what the teachers would say and know it to be true, but I couldn't

137

conceive it. It you can't conceive truth, it cannot set you free. This may be a generational curse standing in your way. You can't achieve things if you don't conceive them. I knew it, but I couldn't express it as knowledge because of the trauma that I was under. I knew truth, but couldn't translate it because of the fear that reminded me of my ignorance. The generational curse encouraged me to think less of my intellect than God's intentions for me. Remember, when we think less of ourselves, it may be because of what the personality of the generational curse tries to make us believe.

Fear will accelerate ignorance, but faith encourages intellect.

Have you ever rehearsed what you were going to say when asked a question, only to be paralyzed by the question when asked? The paralysis dominated your peace, and you succumbed to failure; the thing that you feared the most came upon you. You thought that this was part of you. In all actuality, it was the personality of a generational curse.

I joined up with a team on a science project once, and instead of participating with the project, I was the one that expected everyone to do their part and mine (sounds like the present day church, doesn't it?). As I typically did, I just kept quiet, and let others around me figure out what to do. Unfortunately, things fell through, and we ended up facing a deadline with nothing produced. At the last minute, I began to share my ideas and the facts I had come up with to the group. It didn't take a hypothesis to prove that the truth was the truth; the truth provides proof enough to be evidence, so we aced the science project, and my group and teacher were astonished at the outcome.

The Bible says that you will have no need of a teacher when you have the Holy Spirit's wisdom (John 14:26, I John 2:27). This wisdom will allow you to be a teacher to all teachers. Recently, I've actually taught this revelation to some of my former elementary and high school teachers.

May we pray?

Dear Heavenly Father,

I come to You in the name of Jesus Christ, and repent for any way that I have let the enemy bring forth generational curses in my life that I took on as part of who I am. I repent for the way that I have judged myself wrongly for the personalities that were manifesting because of what my ancestors neglected spiritually. I forgive my ancestors for not paying closer attention to the curses that were evident in their lives, and as a result, they came down to me as an inheritance. I release myself from any and all generational curses that thought that they would control my past, present or future condition concerning the blessings of the Lord. Lord, I seek your truth to set me and my children free from all tormenting, terrorizing, and tempting spirits that come to steal, kill, and destroy. I bless all of my generations back to Adam and speak blessings over all of my future generations in Jesus' Name.

NOTES

NOTES

CHAPTER 9

UNVEILING AND BREAKING CURSES

The breaking of generational curses is the easiest thing to do because the blood of Jesus has the power to break the curse when identified. The hardest part of breaking a generational curse is identifying the curse and calling it for what it is. When you ***get over yourself,*** you automatically walk in a place of freedom that has the power and authority to unveil generational curses. A lot of people don't want to think that generational curses exist, but that has nothing to do with the fact that they do! I told an atheist friend of mine one time that whether you believe in God or not doesn't have anything to do with the fact that He is real. It's kind of like the old saying, "Out of sight, out of mind." This mind-set continues to keep people in the dark about generational curses. Okay, just think about this: if the devil can *"keep you in the dark,"* darkness is a curse.

Generational Curses come to steal, kill and destroy. If not broken, they become greater every generation. However, they can skip a generation or two to gain the extra power needed to take out multiple people at one time. The longer a curse is ignored, the greater it becomes. Unusual happenings that repetitiously occur can often be identified as a curse. A pattern of repetitious destruction, better known as "bad luck," can also be identified as a generational curse. Webster's dictionary defines a *'curse'* as "evil or misfortune that comes as if in response to imprecation or as retribution." Let's take a look at what the Word says about the cause of a curse:

Like the sparrow in her wandering, like the swallow in her flying, so the causeless curse does not alight.

Proverbs 26:2-3, AMP

A curse does not come without a cause; usually the effect is the evidence of the existence. The effects that we have been under for years try to convince us that this is all that there is to life. The Word of God says that Jesus came that we may have life more abundant (John 10:10). If you think that this is all there is to life, you might want to consider metamorphosing. In my brokenness, I thought that this was all life had to offer. But since I've been transformed by the glory of God, every day is a new adventure. Life needs to be an adventure, not something that is dreaded daily. Quit listening to your old perceptions of life and lean into the revelation of God that will fulfill your empty longing to live joyously.

Revelation will always escort confirmation.

Revelation will renew you from your old ways and introduce you to His way. This is also the way that He reveals generational curses. Revelation unveils hidden curses of destruction. Revelation is God's direction and correction from things in life that would cause you harm. Remember, you must not lean on your understanding but learn to lean on His understanding, which is revelation. As God's revelation sets us free from the confusions of false intimacies and heals us by way of true intimacy, His revelation also takes us into a life of liberation from the curses that have kept our destiny hidden.

Curses come to steal your destiny and keep you in a place of seclusion from the truth because the enemy knows the impact that you will have on others if you get free. God's revelation reveals truth in order to set you free, but as His truth comes forth, you must discern that it is Him and not just some crazy thought that's running through your head. As you walk in your healing and wholeness, generational curses will be unveiled in your presence, because when you walk in truth, a lie cannot hide.

You may say, *"How do I hear Revelation?"*

1. Close your mouth long enough to hear Him (God gave us two ears and one month for a good reason)
2. Repent of your own thoughts (your thoughts are not His thoughts)
3. Lean unto His thoughts (have faith to hear what He is saying)

It's that's easy! I can tell you, however, the revelation that what He shares with you has to be understood as His Words and not the words of man. You'll never hear God speak fresh revelation to you that someone else has ever said. Don't get the newness of revelation mixed up with your own personal perceptions of self-doubt and rejections.

Nevertheless, it is the root and the seed of the curse that we seek to destroy and put an end to this evil harvest. Thorns and thistles were not a part of the original plan. They came with the curse. It's time that we live in the garden atmosphere that God created before the fall. You may say, "Is this possible?" I believe that all things are possible. I would rather take my chances on life rather than on death. There is power in the tongue; therefore, we must speak the truth, seek the truth, and live the truth. I've spent my whole life in the desert. I now want to live in the garden.

Life Is Supposed To Be A Vacation, Not A Curse

When we go on vacation, it usually takes half of our time to unwind from the busyness of life. By the time we unwind, it's time to go home. We need to learn to unwind here on earth, before it's time to go to our eternal home. Vacations are a form of visitations. We need to learn how to live life as a vacation. On vacation, you usually do things that you don't normally do in everyday living. You take more chances, you wear different clothing, heck, you might even go out dancing! Whatever the case, vacation is where it is happening, right? Try living life this free and

143

see what happens. Who knows, maybe you will end up installing a mini-golf course in your back yard!!!

This is exercising metamorphosing.

The most difficult part of breaking a curse is allowing the glory of God to bring forth His revelation to reveal the hidden mysteries of curses that have been concealed for generations. After this takes place, then the blood of Jesus applied to the curse finalizes the completion. Curse Broken!

I would like to share a few glory stories about generational curses that have been broken in our ministry:

One afternoon my mother was leaving my home with my children, and as I was seeing them off, there was an explosion out in the middle of the road. The road filled with a bluish white smoke that floated down to the neighbor's house. It sounded like a sonic boom that actually shook the very atmosphere.

My neighbor who lives across the street came out on his front porch and shouted, *"What was that?"* I replied, *"I'm not sure."* As I started walking down the street to see if I could tell what had happened, my mother advised me not to go any further. Curiosity got the best of me, so I decided to act as if I didn't hear my mother's instructions. Nothing was evident of any sort of explosion in the road. The smoke had cleared and everything went back to seemingly normal (well at least for the next 30 minutes).

I was sitting on the front porch with a friend of mine, when two other friends pulled up in somewhat of a panic. The two ladies were mother and daughter, and the daughter was having difficulties breathing. When I asked them what the problem was, they said that she felt as if she was unable to breathe. I began to pray and seek God's face for revelation on this situation, and seemingly, the more I prayed, the worse she became. To make things worse, she was five months pregnant. This went on throughout the night, and things did get worse before they got better (they usually do).

Deliverance came sometime in the midnight hour when the Lord gave me revelation. I told the mother that the generational curse of premature death that came in on the father's side had been broken over her daughter, and that the evidence of the explosion brought confirmation of closure. I then asked the mother how and when did the grandfather die, and she said that he had died at the age of twenty-nine and had been killed by an explosion, and the great-grandfather died at the age of forty-nine. It actually skipped the third generation, but was going to take out two people because of the pregnancy. Generational curses always have to manifest in the same manner that they come to destroy.

The death angel and the glory of God collided and manifested as an explosion.

Another generational curse that was broken is Ernie's story. Ernie is the husband of my Product Manager, Ann. One afternoon Ernie began to have a high fever that needed the attention of the local emergency room. Ann took him, assuming that he may have the flu. To their surprise, the test that was run determined that he had a malfunction with his gall bladder. Unfortunately, it was a little more complicated than expected: gallstones had lodged within his bile duct and apparently had been this way for quite some time.

Suddenly, the surgeons realized that Ernie's situation was a bit more serious than previously previewed. The gall bladder was infected with gangrene. The infection was very angry and the surgeons agreed to immediately open Ernie up. The incision was as aggressive as the infection. This posed another problem for Ernie: the dimensions of this monstrous incision consisted of eighteen inches across, three inches wide, and three and a half inches deep.

Our situations are usually a bit more serious than previewed.

During the process of removing this diseased organ, another unexpected event occurred. The gall bladder disintegrated when the surgeon tried to extract it from the body. The surgeons told Ann afterward that time would tell of the final outcome. Three weeks went by with many more complications that questioned his welfare: one of which left his incision openly exposed because of infection and swelling. At one time, what seemed minimal was now considered detrimental.

I had never met Ernie and needed to make a visit, especially for Ann. At this time, Ann wasn't sure if Ernie was going to live or die, according to the expressions of the surgeons. I wanted to go, but something in me hesitated. Several of our ministry team members wanted to go along with me and became agitated that I couldn't tell them when or what time. I felt as if the Lord had a designated time for us and I had to be sensitive to His plan.

One evening, I was in the shower when the Lord gave me my orders. The Lord instructed me that Ernie was dying, and then suddenly, the glory and power of God manifested upon me. When I came out of the bathroom, I had so much of God's power upon me that I literally felt as if I was about to soar. A friend of mine was at my house and asked me, *"What's wrong?"* She said that she had never seen that much power on me at one time. I told her that the Lord had shown me that Ernie was dying. She said, *"What do we do?"* I said, *"I don't know, but I'm going to lie down and seek the Lord."* She agreed to be in prayer. I told her that I would call her if I needed to. She left at 11:00 PM. As soon as I laid down and closed my eyes, **I was in Ernie's intensive care room.**

Remember, I had never met Ernie before so I didn't even know what he looked like. I came up to the left side (my right) of his bed and he was asleep. I knew everything that was going on. The Holy Spirit instructed me to make four points of contact with him. My toes were to touch his toes, my nose to his nose, my belly to his belly, and the palms of my hands to the palms of his hands. The palms of his hands were down over his stomach. The Lord instructed me to turn the palms upward, because

146

the downward position is posture for burial. As I obeyed the Lord and turned his palms upward, I suddenly was extended over him. Every contact point was being made according to the divine instruction that I had received. In what seemed to be a short while, I was back in my bedroom and the clock said 7:00 AM. I was refreshed as if I had been on a heavenly vacation. I began reading the Bible and soaking in what had happened throughout the night.

I was overwhelmed with the fact that the glory of God had allowed me to travel through the portals of time to partake in such an incredible experience. I knew from that point that Ernie would live. I thought to myself that this was something God had blessed me to take part in, and I was extremely grateful. I was having my coffee outside this particular morning around 9:30 a.m., when the phone rang; it was my friend who had been with me the night before. She said that Ann had called and that Ernie had a bad night and was about to go in for another surgery.

Things are not always as though they seem.

Ann said that she needed us to come and be with her because things didn't look good. Four hours later, we arrived at the hospital (in the natural). We walked right through the doors of the intensive care unit and straight to Ernie's room. When we walked up, the nurses were getting Ernie ready to go into surgery. The only side I could get to him on was the left side, and when I walked up to him he smiled and said, *"What took you so long to get here?"* It was the same man that I had spent the night with! Everything in the room was exactly like I had seen it.

<u>What Took Me So Long To Get There?</u>

I've spent my whole life thinking of that old wives tale: *"There's a a pot of gold at the end of the rainbow"*. Therefore, every time I saw a rainbow, I'd wish that I could find the treasure at the end of that rainbow. **This, however, was not the truth.**

The truth is that the rainbow is a promise from God, and if you follow God, you will find a treasure! When you find the truth, the rainbow comes to you. *You are the treasure of His promise.*

Our fears are the very reason that the supernatural is not normal to us. It's funny to me when I talk about the supernatural, people get real busy because they don't want to speak about it. I talk about it anyway, and when signs, wonders and miracles show up, they then realize the power of God. God desires us to demonstrate His power to others, and that makes people uncomfortable. I have battled my whole life against myself in many areas, only to realize that the enemy did not want me to walk in the supernatural realm. You must get over yourself in order to walk in the supernatural. What takes us so long to get here?

I must decrease in the natural to increase in the supernatural.

Back to Ernie's story: Ernie was heavily medicated, so his asking me what took me so long to get there didn't really mean much to anyone else in the room. But I knew what he was referring to because I had been there all night in the spirit, but in the natural it took me four hours to drive. He was being funny and didn't even realize what was going on! We followed him down the hall as his nurses escorted him to the elevator, and then said our goodbyes. We continued on to the waiting room, where I explained to Ann what had occurred throughout the night.

Ann was physically drained and emotionally exhausted. This ordeal was now approaching a monthly milestone. Days in the hospital seem like weeks, so a month, I'm sure, seemed like a year. Ann told me, "Rebecca, I have prayed everything that I know to pray and it seems as if everything is getting worse." Does this sound familiar to anyone? I said, "I know, Ann, but now you will see a difference in Ernie."

<u>Note:</u> When you have prayed all that you know to pray and there is still no change, you might want to ask God to reveal any generational curses.

The Word of God says,

> Ye ask, and receive not, because ye ask amiss, that ye may
> consume it upon your lusts.
>
> James 4:3, KJV

Ann was praying all that she knew to pray, and that was for her husband to live. Ann had already been praying for years that her husband would die to his natural man and live in Christ Jesus. At this point, things seemed a little contrary. The spirit is always contrary to the flesh, as the curse is contrary to the blessing. We must die to our own way that God's way may take precedence.

> For they that are after the flesh do mind the things of the
> flesh; but they that are after the Spirit the things of the Spirit.
> For to be carnally minded is death; but to be spiritually
> minded is life and peace. Because the carnal mind is enmity
> against God: for it is not subject to the law of God, neither
> indeed can be. So then they that are in the flesh cannot
> please God.
>
> Romans 8:5-8, KJV

The curse was manifesting and it had to be broken for Ernie to live. It didn't sink into Ann that I really knew what I was talking about until she felt the presence of our God. I said, "I spent the night with Ernie last night!" She began to weep and said, "Thank You, Jesus, Thank You, Lord." I told her about the experience as she continued to praise God for what He had done. Meanwhile, their daughter walked into the waiting room. Ann introduced her daughter to me, and she explained to me that she never wanted to meet me. Ann had been traveling with our ministry for about six months and experienced many miracles in a short period of time. She would come home after a conference and tell her family about the rare and bizarre happenings. Sometimes if we don't experience these miracles first hand, the testimonies of these manifestations are hard to believe. Kind of like it is now, you hearing Ernie's story!

We have to get rid of our fear, doubt and unbelief before we can walk in miracles.

If you're afraid of the supernatural, you might want to stop reading this book now. The daughter didn't want to meet me because she was uncomfortable speaking of the supernatural. She made the comment that the supernatural was *"spooky"* and began telling me of some dark manifestations that her friends had experienced at the place that they worked. I've come to tell you that the supernatural is not "SPOOKY". What's spooky is what our children are watching on the latest cartoons...

To ease her anxieties, the Lord instructed me to ask her about the things and people that she so loved. As she began talking about the special people in her life, I began to see her fears disappear. She began to express to me that as she left the hospital the night before, she had the feeling that she would never see her father again. I then explained to them that the Lord had given me revelation about a generational curse that was on Ernie's life.

When you get over yourself and get set free, then the Lord can use you not only to break generational curses in your own family's lives, but for other families as well. I didn't know that Ernie had three brothers that had succumbed to an early death. As I began to share the revelation, they told me of the untimely deaths of all three brothers, plus the father and the grandfather. The grandfather and the father were both 57 years old when they died. His three brothers died at 59, 63, and 64 years of age. The curse of premature death had to be broken if Ernie was going to live.

After I started telling her that we needed to break the curse, she shared that she had feared her whole life that someone close to her would die. The personality of the generational curse had terrorized her daily. She had this fear because she was next in line for the curse to manifest, if not

150

broken. She said for me just to pray that the curse would be broken and I said, *"It's not that simple. I cannot break the curse for you; you have to, because it's your family! I will be glad to lead you in a prayer, but ultimately, it's your repentance that will break the generational curse from your forefathers that is on your generation."* She agreed, and so I lead her through a prayer of repentance over herself and her family, and the curse was finally broken. Praise God!

After the prayer, I told her to go and check on her father, and when she did, she found him in his room, free from a premature curse of death. Things changed that day for this beautiful family, and Ernie was at my last conference, testifying and praising the Lord in good health. There are happy endings when curses are broken.

This makes total sense that the curse was manifesting to take Ernie's life prematurely. Ernie is sixty-nine years old, and although he made it through his sixties, sixty-nine is still too young to die.

There is a website that I visit that consists of a national obituary search. After helping people get set free from the curse of premature death, I then search their name on this website. In Ernie's case, in a two week period of the same time frame that Ernie was set free from the curse of premature death, there were a total of seventy-four other men with Ernie's first and last name who died in the United States of America. One of these men was from Florida and had a wife named Ann!

The Truth Shall Set You Free, If You Let It!

I've heard all of my life that threescore and ten was the promise of a man's life. This is not our promise! One hundred and twenty years is our promise according to Genesis 6:3. I went to my cousin's funeral just this past year and heard the preacher say, "Praise the Lord, our brother made it to his promise. He lived a good, long life and died at seventy years of age." **This is not our promise!**

151

We must know the promise before we can walk in it.

I had a lady argue with me about this truth. I began to tell her that it was a curse and that if she vowed with it, then she would succumb to a premature death. She had a son that had died in a car accident in his early twenties. She is now in her sixties and told me bitterly that she didn't want to live to be a hundred and twenty. There again, I began to speak to her about the people that she loved dearly and her fears began to disappear. I was then able to explain to her about the blessings of a long life.

I asked her what a few of her greatest joys were. She said, *"My grandchildren, of course."* I said, *"How much older are you than your grandchildren."* She said, *"Fifty years."* I then said, *"Would you like to see your grandchildren graduate from high school and then college?"* With a smile on her face she replied, *"Oh yes I would."* I then said, *"How about going to their weddings?"* She began to melt with joy about the thoughts of her grandchildren's future. I continued on, and asked her what about the thought of seeing her great-grandchildren born? She agreed that this would be wonderful. So, if she is now in her sixties, then she needs at least another good forty years to see these things come to pass. But if she believes that the curse is her promise, then she only has a few years to go and won't even see her grandchildren graduate from high school. At this time, she was in tears and said,

"Okay, maybe I do want to live."

My grandmother was one hundred and three when she passed away. She died seventeen years shy of her promise. This is possible, people!!! I began telling this lady more about the curse of premature death that the Israelites received for their murmurings and the fact that they just would not walk into the promise land. I told her that threescore and ten was the curse of the Israelites and that I could prove it. (By the way, it was her preacher who conducted my cousin's funeral service.)

Your carcases shall fall in this wilderness; and all that were numbered of you, according to your whole number, from twenty years old and upward, which have murmured against me...

Numbers 14:29, KJV

For all our days are passed away in thy wrath: we spend our years as a **tale that is told**. The days of our years *are* threescore years and ten; and if by reason of strength *they be* fourscore years, yet is their strength labour and sorrow; for it is soon cut off, and we fly away.

Psalm 90:9-10, KJV

This plainly tells us that if we believe the *"tale that is told,"* then we will succumb to a premature death. According to the Webster's dictionary, a *'tale'* is an "intentional untrue report." The tale that is told here is that our promise is only seventy years (threescore and ten), and we make a vow with this lie and hardly even make it to seventy. However, one hundred and twenty years is our promise, according to the Word of God. We are to be the peculiar people that stand out from others with supernatural benefits of longevity. If we are going to tell others what our promises are, we have to know the truth for ourselves.

We must be the head not the tale!!!

And the Lord said, My spirit shall not always strive with man, for that he also is flesh: yet his days shall be an hundred and twenty years.

Genesis 6:3, KJV

With long life will I satisfy him and show him My salvation.

Psalm 91:16, AMP

I call heaven and earth to witness this day against you that I have set before you life and death, the blessings and the curses; therefore choose life, that you and your descendants may live. And may love the Lord your God, obey His voice, and cling to Him. For He is your life and the length of your days, that you may dwell in the land which the Lord swore to give to your fathers, to Abraham, Isaac, and Jacob.

Deuteronomy 30:19-20, AMP

They Say That This Is Halfway

Do we want to live? Are we going to choose the curse of seventy years as our destiny or a full healthy life of one hundred and twenty peaceful years?

I took a good friend of mine mountain climbing to see a waterfall on her sixty-fifth birthday. A good way up the mountain, we stopped to rest on a bench, alongside another lady who was enjoying her day. After taking a brief water break, we began to prepare for the climb ahead. We were moaning and stretching a good bit from the previous ascent, when the lady said, "They say that this is halfway!" We all murmured under our breath, *"halfway?!"* We began to display our distress about the distance that had already been obtained, and the distance that was still to maintain. It was then the lady confessed to us that she was ninety-one years old. My friend looked at me as if God had sent her an angel to tell her that "SHE WAS HALFWAY THERE!!!!"

The reason people normally don't want to live that long is because of their misery. Once you break this curse of premature death, peace comes along with the blessings of a long life. Let us cast off the former way of thinking and cling to the truth which sets us free to live. Generational Curses have to manifest as broken in the same manner they come to destroy. **Disobedience can reopen a generational curse.**

Let us search the Word of God concerning generational curses and see what it says:

154

"And the Lord passed before him, and proclaimed, the Lord! The Lord! A God merciful and gracious, slow to anger, and abundant in loving-kindness and truth, keeping mercy and loving-kindness for thousands, forgiving iniquity and transgression and sin, but Who will by no means clear the guilty, visiting the iniquity of the fathers upon the children and the children's children, to the third and fourth generation.

Exodus 34:6-7, AMP

You shall not bow down to them or serve them; for I, the Lord your God, am a jealous God, visiting the iniquity of the fathers upon the children to the third and fourth generations of those who hate Me, and showing mercy and steadfast love to thousands and to a thousand generations of those who love Me and keep My commandments.

Deuteronomy 5:9-10, AMP

This shows us that generational curses are real, and can be broken through love, repentance and obedience. True obedience is ongoing. Generational curses torment, terrorize, and place time lines on what God would like to do as blessings for His children. Remember, "Lack of knowledge destroys" (Hosea 4:6). To find out more about what curses may be upon your family lineage, seek God and He will fill in any blanks that have been left void in your family matters. As you continue to walk in the secret place, curses have to unveil themselves and manifest as broken in the same manner that they intended to destroy.

Some people want me to seek out their curses for them because most people don't want to do their own lineage homework. I don't mind helping, but it is more intimate if you and God do it together, because He wants to show you supernatural things, just like He shows me. I can tell you right now that you will find things that leave you a bit awe-stricken, but it's the truth that you need to set you free. Don't let the fear of what you may find out about your ancestors keep you from finding out about

155

your ancestors! It's the hidden secrets of the past that need God's revelation to unfold them and as the truth comes forth, it sets you free from them.

Because of the iniquities of the father, you might want to start on your father's side finding answers first. Under the glory of God that His revelation produces, there is no time or distance. Wherever the generational curses begin, God will take you to that place and reveal the hidden mysteries. As you travel back, you will become sensitive to the leading of the Holy Spirit. Issues from your mother's side will also manifest as you can deal with them.

Here is another glory story about a generational curse that was broken on my photographer's life: We were traveling back from North Carolina after a conference. My photographer was in the back seat asleep when this event occurred. We were approaching a major intersection when suddenly our GPS told us to take a right. I was familiar with this area and told my Event Coordinator (who was operating the GPS) that the directions were not correct. Instead of going through the intersection, I took a right and immediately pulled off of the road. I noticed a cross on the side of the road that symbolized a place of someone's death. I got out of the vehicle and observed this monument intensely. The cross had a purple t-shirt draped over the center and a girl's name along with her birth date and death date. The paraphernalia consisted of stuffed animals and balloons acknowledging her recent birthday. The landscaping around the cross was evidence of someone's presence and attention.

I knew that the glory of God was conditioning our atmosphere for His revelation to unveil something that had been concealed for generations. I told my team that was patiently waiting for my return to write down the name that was on the t-shirt. As I called out the name, my photographer sat up from her state of slumber and responded with, *"What was that last name?"* I repeated the last name again and she said, *"Where are we?"* The others in the vehicle explained our location and then she replied, "This is where my mother was raised!"

Immediately, we googled the name that was on the t-shirt and began a holy investigation that would lead us to my friend's deliverance. I asked my photographer if any of her older ancestors were still alive so that we could ask them some questions. She in return called an elderly aunt who held many answers to our questions. We started filling in the blanks that had been left vacant on this family tree for generations.

God's revelation will fill in blanks of our invalidation's.

Remember, invalidations are things that allow our weaknesses to break us down and keep us from being strong. Invalidations allow curses to remain. Strength heals!

We worked on this curse for about six weeks before we saw a much welcomed breakthrough. The young girl that the cross represented was sixteen years old and ended up being the fourth cousin to my photographer. As we studied this family's lineage, we saw a repetitious pattern of destruction that proved to have taken the lives of many prematurely. This curse is now broken in the name of Jesus and will no longer have a cause to light upon this family. The curse of premature death was broken on my photographer's life that day when we thought that we took the wrong turn. The glory light of God has set this family tree free!!!

Always know that as things come up, hang out with them as long as the Lord allows, and He will take you to the bottom of it and set you free. All of these curses can be found in Deuteronomy 28:15-61. Remember, if perversion (which comes from the enemy) is driving the issue, this is the opposite of provision, which comes from God. We need to be careful what voice you listen to, and remember, God speaks in that "still small voice" (I Kings 19:12). Be careful not to blame God for allowing these curses to come upon you. Iniquity is at fault.

Perversion is anything that isn't God's version!

This next glory story is one of my favorites. I was in my salon one afternoon talking with a client, when she began to confess some of her anxieties about her oldest daughter going off to college. She said, *"I can't go on like I am. I've lost ten pounds and stay nauseated most of the time."* I then said, *"How much longer do you want to live with the fear of something bad happening to your daughter? Would you like for me to lead you through some prayers of deliverance?"* She said, *"I would love for you to."* I led her through a simple twenty second prayer of repentance of the fear that something bad was going to happen to her daughter and suddenly, a generational shift occurred. Repentance always brings revelation, renewal and deliverance. She felt a release that brought tears to her to eyes and joy to her heart that didn't need a verbal explanation, only rejoicing. When she left my salon that day, she was definitely different than she came. When you experience the glory of God, you will always leave differently than you came.

On her way home, she called me and was so excited about the reel of revelation that God had displayed for her. She said that all of a sudden, she realized why she had been so full of fear concerning her daughter. Almost a century ago, her great-grandmother took her grandmother to school one day, and on her way home, was killed by a train as she was driving across the tracks. The grandmother grew up without her mother, but with the fear that something too would eventually happen to her or others that she loved. She taught this fear to her children and then her grandchildren, which were the anxieties of my client's concern.

My client, who happened to be driving down the road, said to me, *"I realize now why I have this fear. It was taught to me by my mother and grandmother.* She was amazed at how God had spoken to her. During her conversation she said, *"Oh my goodness, there has been a bad wreck."* Then she began to scream out her daughter's name over the phone. It was her daughter's car that was upside down and totaled in the woods. I had already started shampooing another client at this time, but I ran out of the salon to go see about them both.

When I arrived, I saw the two of them standing on the side of the road and miraculously, she only had one scratch. The State Patrol said, *"Six out of ten cars that are flipped end in fatalities."* I went down to the upside down car and the radio was still playing. I called the mother down to the car to hear the song that was playing and we heard, *"Wherever you go, God will send angels to watch over you."* She knew that day that the generational curse really had been broken. The very moment we were praying back at the salon, the curse was manifesting to take her daughter's life. Because we had broken it, it did not have a cause to light upon her offspring. **Glory to God!**

**Remember, generational curses will always manifest
in the same manner that they come to destroy.**

Here is a list of a few of the different generational curses, which can help you sort out and/or identify some curses in your life.

Generational Curses

- Curse of Abandonment
- Curse of Rejection
- Curse of Prostitution
- Curse of Hatred and Self-Hatred
- Curse of Bitterness and Self-Bitterness
- Curse of Insecurities
- Curse of Hopelessness
- Curse of Poverty
- Curse of Infirmity
- Curse of Addictions
- Curse of Obesity
- Curse of Insanity
- Curse of Being Incomplete
- Curse of Suicide
- Curse of Divorce

- Curse of Barrenness
- Curse of Confusion
- Curse of Inflammation
- Curse of Depression
- Curse of Fear
- Curse of Dehydration
- Curse of Unloving Spirit

I have plans in the future to write a book with more on this subject. Hopefully, some of this information will enable you to seek out your own deliverance; and who knows, maybe I will be reading your book next!

I will share one more glory story with you before we pray. This is the story of another one of my team members. The curse of self-hatred was broken over this young lady's family, as the Lord gave us the revelation that exposed the root of this curse. Suicide is the highest form of self-hatred. Her brother, who was the third child born, committed suicide. She has a sister whose third child also committed suicide. My friend always feared her child taking his life because of the personality of this curse. The presence of a curse brings forth fear. The fear was present and if not repented of, would allow the curse to manifest. This is what the book of Job says about fear:

Fear is evidence of curses!

For the thing which I greatly feared is come upon me, and that which I was afraid of is come unto me.

Job 3:25, KJV

The thing that we fear the most will come upon us, if we don't repent of the fear, break the curse and be set free. Her fear was that her child would commit suicide, but when she repented of this fear, the curse did not have a place to reside. A few months later there was a little fear that the curse was not broken. This is the enemy's way to try to bring the curse back upon you. The curse was broken, but the enemy tried to torment her with the thought of what if it wasn't. This is what the Lord instructed me to tell her. **"I AM the roll to your scroll."** I didn't really understand this until the Lord gave me more revelation concerning it. When a scroll is unrolled and decreed, then the next step is to roll it back up and file it as history (HIS STORY). In other words, we have to trust that Jesus is the roll to our scroll and file it as finished. We prayed with my friend and she allowed God to roll up the scroll for the last time concerning this curse. It is finished.

> You shall also decide and decree a thing, and it shall be established for you; and the light [of God's favor] shall shine upon your ways.

> Job 22:28, AMP

MY STORY FOR HIS GLORY
HIS STORY
HISTORY

Dear Heavenly Father,

I repent for any and all ways that I have allowed generational curses to operate in my life. I also repent for the way that my ancestors allowed these generational curses to affect our lineage. I ask You, Lord, to restore all areas of my life that these curses have interrupted. I ask that You place the cross between me and any generational curse that tries to hinder me. I repent of any and all fear that would tell me that I am not free and that these curses will one day come back to torment me. I thank You, Lord, for giving me the revelation to unveil hidden mysteries that the adversary had planned against me to keep me from my wholeness. You are such a wonderful God and I love You so. Please reveal any and all other curses that may be upon me and/or my family that I may break them in Jesus Name.

NOTES

CHAPTER 10

THE GLORY
(The Lost Treasure Of The Church)

The Lord showed me that day at the well that I needed His glory to reveal my true purpose in life and to illustrate eternity here on earth. If I was going to be used in these last days, I must have the glory to pull down heaven from my earthly position of authority. The only qualification to carry His glory is that *"I have to be over myself."* He also told me that it was His glory that His children needed to find their true identities as His children, to desire His heart. The Book of Malachi talks about the children's hearts being turned back to the Father's.

We have to find our lost heritage, ourselves and God. We have been the lost treasures of His heart! It only makes sense that if we have been the lost treasures here in this world, then the glory has been the lost treasure in the church. When I say lost treasure, I mean our inner beauty and splendor that God gave us to captivate and illuminate others for His glory and purpose to come forth. The glory turns our ashes into His beauty. We must find who we are in Him regardless of everything that we have been through that tried to prove otherwise. We must find the lost treasure of the church! Remember, we are the church!!!

God created us by His glory for His glory and to be His glory here on earth. If we don't recognize His glory, we sure won't ever recognize ourselves as a carrier of His glory. Remember, you can't give what you don't have. Many ministers of the gospel minister out of their brokenness and pain due to the fact that they themselves have not found this place that the glory has revealed. I call this the secret place of the Most High God. That's why so many people get hurt in the church because ministers tell us what we are supposed to be doing, only to succumb to the same entrapment that they warn us about. This is not always the case, but **"it takes the free, to set the captives free!"** The glory of God sets us free from ourselves where we can help set others free.

The day that I got over myself at the well was the first day that God introduced me to His glory. That day I realized that it was my brokenness that was keeping me from seeing God's glory. I first had to admit that I was a mess and in a great need for a miracle. I never knew about the glory of God before that day. We must be introduced to His glory or we will never know what it is or what it is able to do for us. I would hear songs about the glory but never made any kind of association with the glory because I had never experienced it before.

It was as if scales dropped off of my eyes that day (I can remember my eyes actually itching like crazy for weeks afterwards). The veil had been removed and I could see for the first time into the Spirit realm who I really was. The glory not only revealed the hidden well, it had also unveiled me, the hidden treasure. The glory reveals hidden places in our lives that unveil who we were created to be. The veil of brokenness has to be removed by the glory of God before He can veil us with His glory.

When I was unveiled, I could see beyond anything and beyond everything that I ever had thought or ever imagined. I saw beyond my brokenness and into my wholeness and it was the fact that I got over myself that I experienced this internal/eternal exchange. It was glorious! I have never really liked myself, much less was ever able to love myself. At this moment, I was able to finally love me. It was like I had met myself for the very first time. First impressions are the most powerful!

I don't know how you feel about yourself, but I had been against myself my whole life. I was finally born again, a new creation. Everything seemed different, even the colors in the atmosphere were brighter. As the beams came down from the sunlight, I actually saw light within the beams of the light. It was as if the light itself also had light within it. It was alive, and I was more alive than I had ever been. I could breathe a full breath now, where before I would take shallow breaths. I really knew now what the Bible meant when it referred to us being a new creation.

When I became saved fifteen years ago, people told me that I was born again and a new creation in Christ Jesus, but I never really felt like either. But now, I felt like everything that I had read about in the Word that I thought had nothing to do with me, now it was what He had done for me! For the first time in my life I felt like the butterfly and not the worm. I truly had been born again. At this particular time, I really didn't understand the glory, but now that I have experienced it more, I realize that this is "life more abundant" that the Word of God speaks of in John 10:10.

The Webster's dictionary defines '*glory*' as "great beauty and splendor; magnificence; a state of great gratification; a ring or spot of light; or a halo appearing around a shadow of an object." This is my definition of the glory:

"THE UNEXPLAINED MANIFESTED PRESENCE OF GOD"

When God shows up, He doesn't have to explain Himself. Remember He is God. He doesn't have to get the deacons' vote to show up! Don't expect God's glory to show up replicated to someone else's experience. God's glory has something special for you as an individual and then you can share it with others. God wants to do things in you that He has never done in anyone else. He wants to tell you things that the angels don't even know of.

I had experienced giving God the glory in praise and worship before, but I had never experienced the glory itself coming down upon me that I could see myself as the great beauty and splendor of God. It was one of the most incredible experiences that I have ever had in my life. I even remember thinking a day or two after this experience, that this was something that would not last for very long. You know that old saying, "good things don't last forever." It has now been eight hundred and sixty-four days since this encounter. **Glory to God!**

I have actually seen the glory fill the building where I'm preaching. There has been several times that the glory would get so thick that I couldn't clearly see the people sitting in the congregation. The glory of God comes down in a mist or a sprinkle in our services that other people have also testified of experiencing. The latter rain is greater than the former rain.

The Word of God in Malachi 4:2 says, *"But unto you who revere and worshipfully fear My name shall the Sun of Righteousness arise with healing in His wings and His beams, and you shall go forth and gambol like calves [released] from the stall and leap for joy" (Amplified)*. This was one of the first scriptures that the Lord gave me after the glory began manifesting around me. The glory of God was manifesting as rings and spots of light in the photos that we would take during the renovation of the children's home. At first, I thought that it was just dust particles showing up in the pictures, and then I realized that it looked too brilliant to be dust. It was dust all right, heavenly dust from eternity!

One of my upcoming books will have these photos available, along with testimonies of signs, wonders, and miracles that followed after the glory dust showed up. As the Lord gave me revelation about the glory falling at the children's home, I then began to acknowledge the glory for what it was and it became greater.

We have some really neat pictures of the glory of God coming down on a man who was putting up a fence at the children's home. The Lord impressed me to go over, sit down beside the man and just listen to him as he worked. He began to tell me about his wife of many years and the fact that they never had any children. Then he began telling me about his dogs, along with photos of them on his phone. He seemed to be really

166

proud of his wife and dogs. After that, he began telling me how old he was, along with the age of his business, which was quite impressive. He said the only thing that was ailing him was the arthritic condition of his shoulder and knee. As he explained each afflicted area of concern, he also gave an awful facial expression as confirmation of his condition.

Suddenly, God's glory began to manifest in the background with the colors of the rainbow. I told one of my children to go get the camera to capture this glorious occasion. Glory smoke filled the atmosphere. As soon as she began taking pictures, the glory of God manifested as a huge rainbow right beside him and beams of light in the shape of swords came out of the heavenlies. The swords pierced the area of his painful concerns and he was healed right then and there.

**Having church without the glory of God is like trying
to have a wedding without a bride.**

His Glory Comes Forth, To Reveal Who You Are To Yourself!

When I was at the well, the glory of God settled down upon me the instant I got over myself. God revealed Himself to me that day, which brought forth His glory. As long as I held onto my past pains and brokenness, I disabled myself from obtaining the very substance that not only would heal and set me free, but it would also set nations free. The agonizing substance of my past was so intense that I made vows with the idea that it was better than nothing, and even though it was painful, at least I could feel.

We were made to have emotions! Unfortunately, because of our brokenness, instead of us having emotions, our emotions have us. The Word of God in Ecclesiastes 3 speaks about having a time for every matter or purpose under heaven; TO EVERYTHING there is a season. As I read Ecclesiastes, I'm reminded by the Holy Spirit to discern my emotions like I discern spirits, to see whether they are good or evil.

167

Whatever I invest in emotionally is what I become! Solomon wrote Ecclesiastes out of his negative emotions. His emotions had him!

> Beloved, believe not every spirit, but try the spirits whether they are of God: because many false prophets are gone out into the world.

1 John 4:1, KJV

If our emotions are not lining up with the fruits of the Spirit that are found in Galatians 5, then we might want to discern our emotions. True Intimacy (Love) is what ultimately produces the fruits of God's Spirit. If our emotions are hindering us from producing these fruits, we might want to consider getting healed. I didn't realize how broken I was until the glory of God began manifesting upon me and exposed the hidden intentions of my unhealthy emotional issues. Thank You, Lord, for your Glory!

> And the glory (majesty and splendor) of the Lord shall be revealed, and all flesh shall see it together; for the mouth of the Lord has spoken it.

Isaiah 40:5, AMP

Why wouldn't the glory manifest after His Word says it, and we would see it together? The problem that we have had is that we don't recognize the glory of God like we should, or it would manifest more than it does. The Lord revealed it to me when I began walking under the glory cloud after my experience at the well. One of the first times that I experienced the glory, I was sitting in an office in Alaska and saw beams of light flood through the window unlike any other time that I had ever seen them. They were alive and it was as if they came to minister to me.

Have you ever heard the statement, "shed some light on the subject?" This was actually happening to me. The light of God's glory was shedding truth and deliverance upon me that changed my very being. The Lord impressed upon me,

"Did I change or did you?"

I actually forgave myself for the first time ever and I was able to see His glory. As long as you have unforgiveness, self-judgment and self-bitterness, you will never see His glory like He intends for you to. I released myself through repentance and forgiveness, and my eyes saw the light of God differently. Instead of seeing dimly, I saw clearly for the first time, and I loved it.

> Because of this our hearts are faint and sick; because of these things our eyes are dim and see darkly.
>
> Lamentations 5:17, AMP

> But you are a chosen race, a royal priesthood, a dedicated nation, [God's] own purchased, special people, that you may set forth the wonderful deeds *and* display the virtues and perfections of Him Who called you out of darkness into His marvelous light.
>
> 1 Peter 2:9, AMP

The Appearance Like The Bow

When the sunbeams flooded into the window, I actually saw light within the light (life within my life). We also see the light of God's glory manifest in colors around The House of David. At first I thought that I was going crazy, until other people began to see the same things and together, we saw the glory of God. Thank God for witnesses. I like the way that Ezekiel explains it in the Book of Ezekiel.

Light within life.

Like the appearance of the bow that is in the cloud on the day of rain, so was the appearance of the brightness round about. This was the appearance of the likeness of the glory of the Lord. And when I saw it, I fell upon my face and I heard a voice of One speaking.

Ezekiel 1:28, AMP

For with You is the fountain of life; in Your light do we see light.

Psalm 36:9, AMP

This describes the glory of God manifesting in colors as in the rainbow. We see it as unexplained lights in and around the children's home. At first, people thought that I was crazy, until they saw it appear and were amazed at what they saw. I'll be talking more about the glory in one of my upcoming books, with pictures to prove its existence.

Ezekiel said, "This was the appearance of the likeness of the glory of the Lord. And when I saw it, I fell upon my face and I heard a voice of One speaking." Luke also explains this appearance.

And *behold*, an angel of the Lord stood by them, and the glory of the Lord flashed *and* shone all about them, and they were terribly frightened.

Luke 2:9, AMP

The glory of God desires to manifest more for us, but we must first acknowledge it, and then it becomes greater. The Word of God says:

But [the time is coming when] the earth shall be filled with the knowledge of the glory of the Lord as the waters cover the sea.

Habakkuk 2:14, AMP

The glory of God desires to manifest more for us.

We must acknowledge the glory of God. The Word of God constantly speaks about the light of His glory, but we must learn of His glory and then begin to acknowledge His glory where He can fill us as the waters cover the seas.

> And God said, Let there be light (glory); and there was light (glory).
>
> Genesis 1:3, AMP (paraphrase mine)

> And He Who sat there appeared like [the crystalline brightness of] jasper and [the fiery] sardius, and encircling the throne there was a halo that looked like [a rainbow of] emerald.
>
> Revelation 4:3, AMP

Many times we would see the sunlight reflecting upon the walls through the windows and begin to acknowledge God's glory, and jewels would form in radiant colors. This projection of God's glory brought forth heavenly conversations for those who would visit. We have people travel from all over the place to sit in this majestic atmosphere. My four year old son will often rejoice through the hallway of the children's home, testifying of the glory as it appears.

> Clothed in God's glory [in all its splendor and radiance]. The luster of it resembled a rare and most precious jewel, like jasper, shining clear as crystal.
>
> Revelation 21:11, AMP

I found through this experience that the more I acknowledged the glory (through these manifestations), the more I had to repent of unbelief and doubt. I had to remove the veil of unbelief and doubt, and then the glory became greater. We can't see the light if we continue to be covered by past pains of darkness. Doubt brings darkness! Faith brings forth illumination!

> And all of us, as with unveiled face, [because we] continued to behold [in the Word of God] as in a mirror the glory of the Lord, are constantly being transfigured into His *very own* image in ever increasing splendor and from one degree of glory to another; [for this comes] from the Lord [Who is] the Spirit.
>
> · 2 Corinthians 3:18, AMP

Acknowledgment of the glory enables it to come forth speedily.

When I first began to walk under the glory cloud, I had a few friends over for the weekend. This was all new to me, but I wanted to share what I had experienced. I took a gamble on sharing this with my friends, chancing their rejection. I testified of the unexplained lights appearing on the walls, and how the glory would magnify, once acknowledged. After five hours of explaining this, I wasn't really sure if it was received. But God is always a God of confirmation!

The glory of God suddenly appeared on the wall in streaks of red lights. When my friends saw this, they were amazed. We actually have them experiencing this manifestation on video. I stood back and let them explore the glory of God as it displayed itself from heaven. I told them that if they would acknowledge the glory and thank God for allowing them to experience this, that the lights would become greater. As they excitedly acknowledged Him, the lights grew and began to pulsate in the rhythm of a heartbeat. God is so good! Meanwhile, I was in the background wiping the sweat from my brow, rejoicing that God had been so gracious to manifest Himself in that manner.

The next day, they testified and showed pictures of this manifestation to their pastor, Lemuel Miller, who instantly invited me to share with his congregation about the glory. We had four action-packed services where signs, wonders, and miracles manifested as a result of the glory of God.

As stated in the scripture below, the angels are very aware of the glory of God that is here on this earth. We need to be more like the angels and acknowledge how the earth is filled with His glory.

> And one cried to another and said, Holy, holy, holy is the Lord of hosts; the whole earth is full of his glory.

Isaiah 6:3, AMP

This scripture is from a seraphim's point of view. The angel said that the whole earth was filled with the glory of God. God not only filled *us* with His glory, but the whole earth as well. Adam experienced the glory of God daily in the garden, but when the fall came about, Adam walked away from the glory. He partook of the fruit from the tree of knowledge of good and evil. This caused a veil of ignorance to come upon us. And now we must, through discernment, find and acknowledge the glory, and choose good over evil to allow the glory to move us into the new creation.

We must realize that there is more to the manifestations of God than we have been accustomed to in our normal church services. The glory of God will bring forth manifestations that are sure to take you into your destiny.

If God says that a duck can pull a truck, then I'm going to
HOOK HIM UP!!!

One thing that I have learned about the glory of God is when it comes, it expands you. It expands your faith in great measures. The Word of God says that miracles, signs, and wonders follow those that believe (Mark 16:17-18). If there are no miraculous manifestations, there must be a great deal of unbelief in the atmosphere. There has to be a form of repentance before a supernatural level of faith can come forth (repenting of fear, doubt, and unbelief). Remember, transfer takes place before transplant! So many times we have the mentality of, *"Bless me Lord, indeed and enlarge my territory,"* only to freak out when our territory begins to expand, because it takes more faith to operate. I asked for the Lord to expand me and my territory, and my foot grew a whole size larger! Now that's what I call expansion!!!

The glory of God will also grow you. I asked the Lord to add length to the legs of my friend who desired to be taller. As of the last measurement, she has expanded an inch and a quarter. If we desire to see more manifestations of God's glory (which brings forth miracles), then we must repent for the way that we have let justification take the place of sanctification. We must trade our fears in for a new level of faith. As long as we allow our fears to be a part of our foundation, then faith will not have a place to reside. The glory of God comes to expand us and take us to the next level of glory. Ask God to help your unbelief and expand your faith to see His glory revealed. Be ready to grow though!

Faith will grow us!

A form of repentance is a model in which we need to become accustomed to, just as natural as water flowing in a river. Things have to flow before they can grow. Our availability to flow is what brings forth an atmospheric pressure that recycles the water through spiritual evaporation, and then releases it once again through clouds that transfer aquatic wealth to us at our most desperate times of spiritual drought. Miracles are recycled blessings.

> Then shall we know, *if* we follow on to know the Lord: his going forth is prepared as the morning; and He shall come unto us as the rain, as the latter *and* former rain unto the earth.
>
> Hosea 6:3, KJV

You have to let go to grow!

174

God's Imagery Is Greater Than His Elements

God's glory is in His elements. Fire, water, wind and earth are all expressions of God, which all hold His glory. Expressions are different than imagery. We are imagery of God (Gen. 1:27). *'Image'* is defined in Webster's dictionary as "a visual representation of something." We are representation of Him; His glory enables us to become a replica of Him. Imagery is reflecting who He is in us! So therefore, we are created by His glory to behold His glory, which qualifies us for His greater glory. Jesus said, *"Greater things shall you do, than I" (John 14:12)*. We are called to reflect His imagery. If a reflector is broken, then it projects brokenness. A reflector has to be whole before it can cast forth the light that is received. The glory of God comes to make us whole, then we can be that glory reflector to help others find wholeness as well.

We must first realize that we are greater than the elements. Elements are expressions of God. We are imagery. His imagery is greater than His elements. He created the elements for our enjoyment. Since the fall of man and the fact that we have been displaced by our dysfunctions, there has been an interruption between man and the elements. Jesus, when walking on the water, scared the disciples because they had never seen such power, that one could have authority over the elements. When Jesus spoke to the winds, they also obeyed Him. Peter caught hold of this example of authority for just a moment, as he stepped out of the boat and began walking on the water. These are some examples of taking authority over the elements and knowing that you (God's imagery) is greater than God's expressions.

I teach a Bible study every Wednesday in my hometown. People come from all over to sit in at least eight hours of straight revelation from God. One particular day, I happened to be teaching on the revelation that God gave me about His imagery is greater than His elements. We have to come to this realization that we are greater than the wind! I know its hard to believe, but how about believing that you are greater than fire!! Or how about this one, more powerful than the earth or water?

I taught all morning on how we were greater than the elements. I noticed that it was getting a little dark outside and the wind began to blow. There was no storm warning in the forecast. My phone rang and it was my father instructing me to take the bible study group to the children's home about 6 miles away, where they would be safe. My brother also called and said that there had been a tornado sighted and to take cover. It was if there was a showdown in the atmosphere from what I had taught the people.

I began walking around the property and repenting of any fear, doubt and unbelief that would hinder me from taking authority over the wind element. Every time I would circle the building my students were in, they would just look at me, waiting to see the outcome of this adventure. The winds and rain came forcefully along with a few limbs, but ultimately the storm ceased and a calm covered my land and the people witnessing this event. Later, a man testified that a tornado was heading towards our county but as it approached our area it disintegrated off of the radar. **Glory to God.**

I often hear people express their opinions of natural disasters. I've heard Christians say before that, "it was the wrath of God that destroyed that city or state." I beg to differ!!! The Bible speaks of the wrath of God, but I don't believe that we have experienced it as of yet. If it were the wrath of God, we would all be destroyed. You might want to reconsider judging these cities or states out of false accusations that were formed from your ignorance. What are the chances of you ministering to the people of these disaster areas that God loves them and desires to protect them, if you think that His wrath caused the disaster? Let's be real careful not to say anything when we really don't know the answers.

I believe that if the remnant of God's people would rise up and take dominion and authority over the elements, then disaster would not have a chance in hell!!! We are greater than the elements, but if we do not take authority, the elements become greater than us. What we don't take authority over, takes authority over us!

Here are a few scriptures to back up this revelation that God gave me concerning His imagery being greater than His elements.

- Shadrach, Meshach and Abednego in the fiery furnace. (Dan. 3)
- Peter walking on the water (Matthew 14:29).
- Jesus walking on the water (Matthew 14:25).
- Jesus spoke to the winds and they obeyed Him (Mark 4:39).
- Samson exercised his authority over the rock pillars when he pulled them down (Judges 16:29).
- Elijah calling down the fire to lick up the water around the trench (1 Kings18:38)
- Elijah's servant calling forth the rain (1 Kings 18:44).
- Moses parting the sea (Exodus 14:21).
- Moses turned the bitter waters sweet (Exodus 15:25).
- Moses struck the rock and brought forth water (Exodus 17:6).
- Elisha cleansed the water by using salt (2 Kings 2:21).
- Elisha made the ax head float (2 Kings 6:6).
- Elijah smote the waters and they divided (2 Kings 2:8).
- Elisha smote the waters and they divided (2 Kings 2:14).

Now that's what I call taking authority over the elements!!!! We must learn in this hour the power that God has given us to operate over the elements. This is also considered a demonstration of God's power to show all of the present day Pharaohs that God is still in control.

God Will Use A Turkey

When you realize that you are greater than the elements and you begin to operate in this authority, don't be surprised if animals are attracted to you. I said attract, not attack! Remember, everything is opposite as it was in the garden. I believe that we can live in this secret place here on earth as it is in heaven. We've been in the wilderness way too long; now it's time to dwell in the garden.

177

When I first started walking in this authority, I thought it a bit strange one day when a wild turkey walked up to me. Me and a friend of mine were at the edge of town close to a wooded area and all of a sudden, I heard this gobbling noise. I began looking around and to my surprise, a huge turkey was walking out of the woods towards me. I was scared at first because this was quite unusual. I started taking authority over my fear and the more I repented, the closer the turkey got to me. I could clearly see the talons on the back of his feet that resemble razors, which stirred up my fear once again. I continued to repent and was very aware of the fact that I had to stay away from my own thoughts as well. My thoughts were telling me that this was not possible and that turkeys don't come to people like this. Remember, God wants us to experience the supernatural! As long as I stayed in a neutral place concerning my emotions and repenting when fear would arise, then the turkey felt comfortable enough to come to me. Normally when I tell this story, people look at me a little strange until I show them the video that we were able to take. Glory to God.

We are imagery of God; His glory is in us. We are greater than the elements, so therefore, whatever He has ever created has His glory. In other words, when we need supernatural assistance, everything around us that He has created has the glory within it. We can call forth the glory of God to manifest, and it instantly comes forth. We don't have to do it alone; His glory is already here to help us out.

We are surrounded with His glory. He says in His Word that if we don't cry out, then He would have His rocks to cry out (Luke 19:40). In other words, what we don't do, He will have His elements do for us. It needs to be natural for us to repent and be willing at any given point to recognize our wrongs. When we can accomplish this form of repentance and seek God's face for forgiveness of our wrongs, then this will bring us into an atmosphere of the supernatural.

If we don't praise Him the rocks will.

The Real Reason it Rained

Let me share a revelation that God gave me concerning one of His elements: rain. The real reason that it flooded was because in the beginning, God gave man dominion over all the elements. A mist came up from out of the ground to give the earth the moisture that it needed to produce fruits and cool man (even God wants man to be cool!). Anyway, when man failed and was evicted from the garden, he lost his position of dominion. After the fall of man, everything became opposite of God's original intention. Example: Before the fall, the lion and the lamb laid down together in peace. After the fall, the lion ate the lamb. Everything in this earth as we know it is opposite to what God intended for man, therefore causing an opposition between the natural and supernatural. The supernatural is supposed to be natural and still can be, if we overcome our fallen state. It is possible to overcome your brokenness where your supernatural life can come forth as natural. This can be a bit tricky, though.

Back to the real reason it rained. The mist came up from the earth to saturate the garden and bring forth growth (life) to all creation. By the way, there was no reason for seasons in the garden of Eden because before the fall nothing ever died. Think about it! Because everything became opposite, the rain came down instead of coming up. It ended up flooding the earth because man lost his rightful position of authority to speak to the element in which he was given dominion. Therefore, what was originally intended to bring forth growth, brought forth death. Repentance brings forth restoration, and that is why we can overcome our brokenness and then take back dominion over the elements of God.

What you don't take dominion and authority over will take dominion and authority over you.

We must learn how to overcome the very thing that displaced us and repent to receive our authority back. We must learn from this lesson of the rain to truly learn how to reign. Royalty reigns! We can no longer afford to be flooded by our unhealthy emotions to the point of destruction. Send out the dove of your repentance and watch him return with the olive branch of peace.

In other words, God didn't take back what He gave man, but man was removed (by his own rebellion) from his position, because he misunderstood his rightful position. God never takes back what He gives, so it is up to us to repent and be replaced in our rightful position of authority. God has given us dominion (even over the enemy), but if we have a veil of ignorance on, which comes from sin and rebellion, then we can't take our rightful position of authority. Authority comes as we understand and learn from our mistakes. It's not a mistake if you learn from it.

We must allow the revelation of God to unveil us to the point that repentance is automatic. Repentance is something that should be offered daily as a sacrifice of our willingness to walk in miracles. It is also an act of humility that always impresses heaven. When we get to this place, it's only then that God uses us as a catalyst to bring heaven down to earth. We must be familiar with the reflecting power-flowing process before we can get to the place of GUSH. Gush will be aborted if we RUSH. We must realign with our rightful kingdom position of power and authority.

Be still and know that I am God (Ps. 46:10).

I always knew that there was more to serving God than just going to church and occupying a pew. I worked with a company out of New York, traveling the United States as a platform artist teaching the art of hair design. I was in my hotel one afternoon, resting before leaving for a corporate engagement, when suddenly, I felt as if the Lord was calling me to go deeper in my commitment level of our relationship. The glory of God filled my room, and I carefully slid off of my bed and onto the floor, because this was unlike any other experience I'd ever known. Somehow, I knew the closer I could get to the floor, the greater His presence would become. I now know this to be a posture of humility.

He began to minister to me that there was more, and the fact that I had been seeking more was the very reason that He came. The Word of God says "if we will draw nigh to Him, then He will draw nigh to us." This was my first experience with the glory of God invading my atmosphere.

The glory of God comes after the anointing of God sets us free to the point of desiring more of Him and less of ourselves. The anointing of God took Jesus to the cross, but it was His glory that took Him from the cross. The very thing that Jesus said on the cross was, *"It is finished."* We need to get to the place that we too say, "This is finished." The anointing has taken us this far, but the glory of God desires to take us on into the places of the supernatural. We must seek to find and knock, before the door can and will be opened.

> He must increase, but I must decrease. [He must grow more prominent; I must grow less so.]
>
> John 3:30, AMP

Knock and the Door will be Opened

I recently conducted a Women's Glory Retreat at a lodge secluded back in the woods. We had planned this retreat for months and were all excited about spending a whole weekend in the glory of God. The idea was to disconnect from our everyday agendas and seek the face of our Father. Well, if we had been planning this for months and were anticipating the Father's arrival at our little get together, how much more excited do you think He was? I feel sure that He was there waiting when we arrived. God is never late. He always shows up early!

A few weeks before this event, the Lord awakened me one morning and impressed upon me to sketch an open door with His fire coming out of the top and water coming out of the bottom. The fire and the water represented two of the elements (remember elements are expressions of

God). The Lord had me to draw the Star of David in the center of the door connecting the two. The colors that encompassed the inner circumference composed the kaleidoscope of creation. God loves colors, and anywhere that color is manifested is a sure sign of life. He will always manifest Himself in the midst of His creation.

The Bible says in Matthew 18:20, *"Where two or more are gathered there He is in the midst."* He also had me to draw an eye in the center of the Star of David in representation of He sees us anyway, so we might as well be truthful to Him in order to be set free. Remember, honesty partners with true intimacy to bring forth healing. At the bottom of this prophetic drawing, the Lord had me to write the words,

"The Door Is Open To See God's Glory."

I immediately took this design to the local print shop and had a glory t-shirt made for the women's retreat. Most all of the ladies purchased a t-shirt upon arrival while registering at the book table. The shirts were worn throughout the weekend, not ever imagining what they were participating in prophetically.

The Saturday night of the retreat, the Lord impressed upon me to give an impartation. While everyone attended the evening meal, I went to prepare myself before the Lord for this glorious impartation. Upon my arrival at the meeting, I cloaked myself with a prayer shawl that disguised who I was, and continued up to the heavy gymnasium-type doors of entrance. My father was escorting me, and as we approached the entrance, the door miraculously opened before us, and the glory of God filled the lodge. People began to weep, and some laid out prostrate before Him, in amazement of Him. I never said a word to anyone. I just laid my hands on them one by one as they came up, and imparted what the Lord had given me, and it was glorious! God allowed me to see with His eyes for at least forty-five minutes, and I can tell you that the way we look at people is nothing like He sees them. The way that we look at ourselves is nothing like He sees us, either!!!

Here is a testimony from my friend Charles, who was running the soundboard that night. He wanted to share what he saw with you.

I guess the whole time since I've been saved, I have never had an open vision. I was in the back behind some ladies, so I didn't see the doors open. All I saw was ladies falling to the floor and weeping. I didn't know what was going on. I didn't know until later, but the floor where she would have us to come walk up to to receive our impartation, was lined with candles. The color of the floor changed when the doors opened, and we've got this on film. It changed from a tan color to royal blue. When I turned to walk up through the candles and looked down, all the lights were down and all I saw was a silhouette. I didn't see Rebecca King, I saw Jesus now. I don't know how good you are or how forgiving you are, but when you come face to face with Him, you <u>will</u> bow your head. I got about 5 feet away, looked and saw great big toes. I'm having this experience, and I said, "Lord Girl, we need to pray about those feet." (chuckle) I saw the toe nail, then I saw sandals... (She had on tennis shoes). Then I saw the ankle, hair on the leg, and all this happened in about 4 seconds. I saw the robe, the bottom of the robe, and when I got to the knee, that's when it came to me: "This isn't Rebecca. This is Jesus." It suddenly turned to blue jeans then. My eyes dropped back to the feet and she had on tennis shoes! The whole time it was a little cloudy, but it was still clear enough to see. I kept it all to myself until after the meeting because I didn't know about the door coming open. All I know is He was there. Other people got to sense His presence. Some got to see the door open; I saw Him. I saw Him. Praise God. Praise the Lord!

Charles

I wish that I had more time to add to this book some more of the testimonies of the creative miracles manifested in the lives of those ladies that weekend, but maybe this too will be an addition to my authorial portfolio.

Truths About God's Glory

The truths of God remind us that greater is He that is in us, than he that is in this world (I John 4:4). The Bible also says that we are to think upon good things (Phil. 4:8). If we allow negative thoughts to bombard our minds and do nothing about them, then we begin to dwindle down to the deception of their delusion. We must be strong and courageous in our thought life to conquer the enemy at hand by taking every thought captive unto the obedience of Christ (II Cor. 10:5). The glory of God is where we have an advantage over the enemy. Remember, the more that you acknowledge the glory, the greater it becomes. We have to have a Caleb and Joshua mentality to overthrow the demise in which the enemy has devised to keep us out of the promises of God.

Before the glory of God set me free, I would take thoughts captive, and once I had them, I wouldn't know what to do with them. It was like trying to tame a wild squirrel! Since then, I've learned how to allow the glory of God to destroy what I capture. In the glory, the enemy's plans are pulverized. The problem was, before, I would take ownership of the thought because of the personality of the generational curse. As long as you take ownership of the thought, it will remain and/or always return. Meditating on the truths of God will remind you that you don't have to put up with the enemy's lies a day longer. The truths that are mentioned in this chapter and the other chapters, if meditated on, will strengthen you and keep you available for freedom.

Here are a few glory truths to help you stay focused:

- The glory of God changes the atmosphere.
- The glory is the unexplained manifested presence of God.
- The glory of God is different than the anointing of God.
- Jesus is the Anointed One, and it was the anointing that took Jesus to the cross, but it was the glory that took Him from the cross. The glory causes a shift in conditions.

- The anointing brings forth visitations, but the glory brings forth habitation.
- It was the glory fire of God that Moses saw on the bush.
- The glory will engulf you, not consume you.
- The glory of God will take you further than you have ever dreamed you could go.
- The Strong's Concordance mentions the word '*glory*' only one hundred ninety-nine times less than the word '*Holy*'. We have put so much emphasis on the giftings that we have missed the glory of God.
- The glory will allow you to hear someone else's thoughts. (Just like Jesus did—many times the Bible says that Jesus knew the thoughts of those around Him).
- The glory will bring you victory over yourself and your circumstances.
- Portals open in the heavenlies when you acknowledge the glory.
- The glory of God is in the elements, which are fire, water, wind and earth. These are expressions of God. However, we are imagery of God, so therefore, the glory in us is greater than the glory in the elements. We must learn this in order to acknowledge our authority over the elements. This was how Peter was able to walk on the water.
- The glory brings revelation, but in order to dwell in the glory, you must get over yourself. The more that you decrease, the more His glory will increase.
- The glory brings restoration.
- The glory manifests to illuminate truth and expose darkness.
- In the glory, there is no time or distance.
- Fear, doubt, and unbelief will disable you from seeing the glory.
- The glory breaks religion and then develops relationship.
- The glory brings change and transformation.
- Under the glory, schemes are exposed.
- The glory will take you to the place of expansion, expansion brings exposure, and exposure makes us transparent. When

transparent, we are able to project the glory that He has placed upon us. Transparency takes place when darkness flees.

- Under the glory you become more accurate than ever.
- The glory comes to promote us, not demote us.
- The anointing brings forth prophecy, and the glory brings forth revelation. The difference between prophecy and revelation is a "now word." Prophecy needs time to come forth, but revelation dominates time. It's a "now word."
- The glory forces you to deal with yourself. His power, splendor, and beauty awakens you to acknowledge your own true inner beauty.
- The glory desires a nest and requires a platform of excellence for your gifts to come forth.
- The glory can manifest as unexplained lights like what you see in a rainbow.
- The glory of God is our only true covering.
- The glory requires acknowledgment. The more that you acknowledge the glory, the greater it becomes.
- The glory has always been and always will be.
- The glory will produce a place inside of a place for you to dwell. (Ps. 91).
- The glory proves itself. All we have to do is obey the atmosphere of His presence, and it brings life.
- We have ownership of the glory because we are made by His authority, but we must always give Him all the glory in order to see the greater glory.
- The glory will take you out to bring you in.
- The glory cannot be touched, just experienced by true intimacy.
- Creation is God's glory in action (Gen. 1:27).
- God's glory will manifest when it is desired. We can come into God's glory anytime, anywhere. We just have to call it forth.
- The glory must be sought after (Matt. 7:7). The more obedient you are, the greater the glory will be (I Sam. 15:22).
- Everything that you have need of is in the glory (John 14:14).

- The glory heals here on earth.
- The glory will manifest as joy, peace, and happiness daily, seven days a week.
- The glory will give you a "new heart" (Ps. 51:10). God's glory takes you back in time to revisit past pains and dissolves the memory of them (Josh. 10:12-13).
- Your past cannot remain powerful under the glory.
- The glory of God allows you to deal with things that you have never been able to handle.
- The glory will set you free (John 8:32).
- The glory changes seasons in the natural and in the spiritual, so don't fight change; it's the glory.
- The glory will hold your hand (Isa. 42:6).
- The glory of God will be seven times greater upon you (Isa. 30:26).
- The glory makes bitter things sweet (Eccl. 11:7).
- The glory brings light to the eyes, joy to the heart, and nourishes the bones (Prov. 15:30).
- The glory makes you see things as they truly are.
- The glory drives out depression and encourages joy (Ps. 43:3).
- The glory will strengthen you to go ahead of your storm (I Kings 18:46).
- The glory of God will fill your house with all that you need (I Sam. 6:12).
- The glory shines brighter and makes things clearer for more understanding (Prov. 4:18).
- The glory illuminates your pathway (Ps. 119:105).
- The glory offers favor and protection (Ps. 97:11).
- The glory reveals the truth (Ps. 43:3).
- The glory is a sure foundation (Ps. 36:9).
- The glory has always been from the beginning (Gen. 1:3).
- The glory is our covering (Rom. 13:12).
- The glory is our rear guard (Isa. 58:8).

- The glory has flavor; "Taste and see that He is good" (Ps. 34:8).
- Creative miracles are in the atmosphere of the glory. A creative miracle is the manifestation of something missing or broken. I have actually seen a spinal column over a woman's head in a picture that was taken after we had prayed for a new spine.
- The glory of God makes you transparent from the enemy. We have pictures of me becoming transparent while preaching.
- In the glory, you see things before they happen. This is not what people call déjà-vu; it is the glory of God in you!
- The glory comes to make you whole.
- The glory manifests greater for seekers and givers. This enables you to become a mover and shaker.
- The glory comes to take you into an intoxicating place of intimacy with Him.
- The glory can quench your thirst.
- The glory can be imparted.
- When you're under the glory, you see things differently and don't take things out on yourself.
- The glory went with Elijah wherever he went, until he allowed self-pity to remove himself from the glory.
- When the glory comes down, it is heaven invading earth.
- In the glory of God, there is no reverse. You only can go forward.
- The glory can't be bought; it has to be birthed.
- When the glory shows up, this means that you are close to His throne and His bosom.
- The glory is waiting on you to realize who you are in Him.
- We have to decree and declare that we release our natural mind to have the mind of glory.
- Under the glory, no one is left behind or excluded. Fear, doubt, and unbelief are the only things that will separate you from His glory.
- When you line up with the glory, the atmosphere around you will come into supernatural alignment.

- In the glory, your expectation is "right now."
- The glory forces you to deal with yourself and face your fears. There is no reason we should tolerate brokenness.
- In the glory, there is the greatest peace that you have ever known.

The glory is our inheritance!

May I lead you in a prayer concerning the glory of God?

Dear Heavenly Father,

We thank You for sending Your only begotten Son, Jesus, to die on the cross for all of our sins, and the fact that we can be made whole by the stripes that He bore upon His body for our healings. You are an awesome Father, and we are grateful to You for all that You sacrificed. We repent for the way that we have not fully taken our position in the power that You made available to us through the process of crucifixion. Your glory has enabled us to accomplish all things and has made a way for us where there seems to be no way possible. The glory has brought us out of our "Egypt of Emptiness" into the "Palace of Overflow" so many times over, and for that, we praise You. You have crowned us with Your glory and set our feet upon the glorious heights far above our foes. We ask you to forgive us for all of our insensitive ways concerning our lack of involvement in Your will and plan for our lives. We submit to You right now all of our wrongs through repentance and agree to conform to a daily model of repentance, to achieve heavenly progress to take place here on this earth. Your will be done in our lives, In Jesus' Name.

NOTES:

CHAPTER 11

MOSES IN THE NILE

Come on, we've made it this far, don't turn back now. Allow me to share with you a parallel that Moses and I share concerning the dreaded dysfunction of denial. Moses has always been an interesting character in the Bible to me. I am amused at his lack of self-confidence, along with the fact that he lived in fear; but then again, he is just a man. The inclination of his speech impediment indicated that there had been trauma sometime in his life. Moses was seemingly under a generational curse of abandonment that postponed his discovery of his true identity for many years. I never remember reading anything that related to his father's presence, other than in Exodus 2, *"Now Amram, a man of the house of Levi, went and took a wife, a daughter of Levi, and the woman became pregnant."* I'm assuming that invalidation was probably an issue as well. Ladies, this is to encourage you that you can help your child even if the father is nowhere in the picture.

His mother placed him in the Nile as a form of protection from death. Moses, however, may have taken this on as a negative emotion of abandonment that impressed a lifelong quest of trying to find truth. He also could have been under a generational curse from his counterfeit grandfather, Pharaoh. False intimacy will try to create counterfeit relationships to prove to you that you have no true identity and no chance of any inheritance.

Moses' mother took a chance on life for her son. Death had been decreed over all the Hebrew male children under the age of two, by the very man that soon became Moses' (adoptive) grandfather. Talking about dysfunctional! Death decrees desire to adopt you. When breaking a generational curse, we must be willing to invest in and take a chance on life when everything around us has seemingly received the declaration of death.

Moses' mother made him an ark (basket) that consisted of twigs of positive thoughts, prayerful papyrus, and unbiased bitumen that was sure to find floating favor from her Heavenly Father.

She unrelentingly released all of her fears that tried to convince her that her son would die because of this declaration of premature death. This demonic declaration of premature death has been rampant ever since the fall of man. Remember, Adam & Eve's son, Abel, was killed prematurely! The available access to life more abundantly requires the activation of the depths of our faith in such a seemingly detrimental derangement. What seemed like was going to take her son's life, her devotion to a Holy God determined otherwise. The glory in Moses was greater than the glory in the Nile, but it was his mother's faith that extinguished the itinerary of his adversary. Moses' mother knew the God of glory because she was able to rely and trust in a God that she had never seen before. This is **Faith**!

Anyone who knows the God of glory acknowledges the glory in other elements as being lesser than, but still more than able to produce miracles. Remember the glory of God is in all the elements around us such as the water, fire, earth and wind. The Word says that everything that has been created was created by Him. She released Moses in the waters of the Nile, knowing that the waters had the power to also bring death to her offspring, not to mention the creatures within the water. Her faith encouraged her to expect the water to support her promise from God, instead of fearing that it too could be the death of him. She put her

192

trust in God and leaned not unto her own understanding and was able to take advantage of the benefits of the glory that was in the water. The glory in the water transferred Moses from his mother's arms into the arms of Pharaoh's daughter. The glory of God will transport you to safety.

As Moses was released into the Nile, this proved her stability in a God that impregnated her very atmosphere with the anticipation of salvation. Faith floats, while fear sinks. There comes a time even in tough situations that you have to make a choice to let go of your fears. She was operating in what I call generational glory; she gave him up and then eighty years later, he saved the whole nation of Israel. Abraham also walked in generational glory when he gave Isaac up at the altar. Generational glory always brings back to you what you unselfishly give up.

Moses was under a fifth generation mantle that was established because his mother broke the curse before it had time to manifest and take any of her children. Moses' mother had to release herself from all denial to be able to place her son in the Nile.

We must release our children from our fears that eventually form denial.

This fifth generation mantle is called the "*Phares mantle*". It is in this place that the mantle falls on our children because we have taken responsibility for the last (which is the fourth) generation of the iniquities of our forefathers. The curse stops here! That puts our children in the numeric lineage of the fifth generation. Phares is found in Matthew 1 as the fifth generation from Abraham. In some translations it is spelled 'Perez.' '*Phares*' in the Greek/Hebrew means "splendor, truthfulness, confidence, evermore, perpetual, strength, victory, end, and constantly." This is exactly what I desire for my children and grandchildren. The fifth generation mantle is the end of ancestral curses, because the blessing of the fifth goes into the thousands, therefore saving many generations of the Abrahamic lineage.

Because of the fifth generational mantle, her children eventually united together to defeat another curse of slavery upon their family. I will be talking more about this mantle in upcoming books. We must realize that in times of extreme trouble, we can call upon the God of our ancestors Abraham, Isaac and Jacob to perform the miraculous. He never leaves us nor forsakes us, and He is here to provide a ram in the thicket for you and your children.

Moses was only three months old when this event took place. His mother's faith proved to be true when a psychosomatic process brought forth evidence that God's promises will come to pass as "yea and amen." I'm sure when Moses was released into the frigid waters of the Nile River, his senses reassured his mind that something definitely had come up contrary to the warm atmosphere that he had been accustomed to. I feel sure that before his mother sent him off, she did what every mother would have done, and that was to provide for him a good meal. As the current of his present situation took him downstream, his voice began to cry out for the very comfort that his mother's breast had offered him of contentment and nourishment.

The act of her faith required the full surrender of her intellect; she cautiously turned her head to cry.

Both she and her offspring were now in the midst of a miracle that desperately needed unfolding. Too many times, we as parents allow our intellect to get in our way and prohibit miracles from coming to pass within our children, when we should get out of the way and allow God's eternal purpose to come to pass. Kingdom knowledge is an understanding of whatever we let go of will come right back to us! As Moses floated down this river of God's provisions, his sister Miriam followed, watching from afar. Meanwhile, Pharaoh's daughter was bathing and caught a glimpse of the baby's presence about the same time she heard his cry. Suddenly, the fate of Moses changed positions and God heard his cry, along with his mother who was left behind on the river bank. Just about the time that things seem impossible, God will hear the

194

cry of His people and provide a way out where there seems to be no way out.

No one is left behind in the glory!

Back to the psychosomatic process! When Moses began to cry as part of his destiny came to pass, his mother heard his cry from up river and her breasts brought forth the promise of milk, and before she knew it, Moses was miraculously back in her arms before mealtime. By the way, not only did God make a way for Moses to return, He also made sure the mother went on Pharaoh's payroll that day!

The Webster's dictionary defines '*psychosomatic*' as "relating to, concerned with, or involving both mind and body." Our mind and body need to line up with the promises of God as He brings forth provisions that float us towards our destiny. When a baby cries, the mother's breasts release the milk that is promised to her child as nourishment. Too many times, we give up and allow our fears to dry up the natural process of God's provisions, because of the unbelief and denial that comes to steal our miracles. Denial is evidence of doubt.

How To Destroy "Denial" Before It Destroys You!

The Webster's dictionary defines '*denial*' as "the refusal to admit the truth of reality." It's the truth of God that sets us free, but if we have denial, then we won't allow ourselves to see or hear the truth. Denial denies revelation. Jesus told the disciples that *"you have ears to hear but you don't hear! You have eyes to see but you don't see!"*

Denial will keep you from hearing and seeing.

If we have denial in our lives, then we have lies in our life! Denial is based on a foundation of deceptions and unhealthy perceptions. People usually get on to their children for lying, but what about your denial?

Who's going to get on to you? That's what this book is for. Repent for operating in denial, consider your ways and ask the Holy Spirit if you have any areas of denial and He will show you the truth. Hang on, this one hurts!!! The truth of God is like getting an adjustment from the local chiropractor, it hurts so good.

The majority of our wholeness is determined by our willingness to destroy denial. The very thing that you think you don't have wrong with you, will be the very thing that you are contaminated with. Evidence of denial is defending broken areas in your life in which you desire to see a difference. As long as we are under the influence of denial, deliverance cannot take its rightful position. Denial is realizing something is wrong, but not knowing what to do about it. Denial is a combination of fear and lack of knowledge. We have been programmed for so long that, "I am fine, don't worry about me," then we get aggravated with others for not worrying about us. This is what we call an oxymoron. We have to drop that *"I'm fine"* mentality, and go in for our ultimate healing.

Denial will keep you from your destiny.

I asked a lady one time (who was obviously in denial) if she had any unforgiveness in her heart. After having to repeat myself because she was deaf in one ear, she argued with me that she didn't have any unforgiveness. She was a bit angry because she thought that I assumed that she did. She had defended her brokenness for so long and protected her false identity of denial that she became angry with me as I spoke the truth. I lead her through a short prayer of repentance, and she forgave herself for having unforgiveness against herself and others. Instantly, her deaf ear popped open, and she has been healed ever since. Praise God.

Her denial had convinced her that she didn't have any unforgivenness, until repentance canceled the debt. Denial is just as deadly as unforgiveness. Denial will also tell you that nothing is wrong with you, when everything is wrong with you. It is an untruth that the enemy uses against us as the counterfeit of truth. Just remember that sometimes, it gets a little sticky speaking the truth. You must always speak the truth bold as a lion and humble as a lamb. If you operate in the lion mode only, then you might have a fight!

The Nile River is a very dangerous place to be, but denial of where you are spiritually is more dangerous than all the crocodiles of the Nile combined.

After Moses had become a man under the influence of the Egyptian ruler called a Pharaoh, who was now actually his grandfather. He began to realize that the very truths that his mother spoke over him before he was weaned became a daily chore of discernment. Moses was saved from the very declaration that Pharaoh made against him, only to adapt to the teachings of a mass murderer.

The day that he stood up for his Hebrew brother determined that he too was a murderer. Suddenly he had an overwhelming passion to protect his own people. This scared him because what was in him came out of him. The Word of God says that out of the heart flow the issues of life. What is in our hearts will eventually come out, whether it be good or bad. Moses was in denial of the power to kill that was embedded within him by his adoptive grandfather. This brought major confusion, and confusion will always encourage you to run.

When we are weaned in truth, then we will always seek the truth in hopes of maturity. Immaturity is evidence of brokenness that will keep you entrapped to hopelessness. We must be willing to go back and retract the very act of any false intimacy that embedded unhealthy emotions within us that would encourage us to cooperate with a generational curse. Moses was not a killer, but the generational curse of Pharaoh was manifesting in his own life now. Generational curses promote denial as a deterrent from one's destiny, and must be broken when they manifest.

Out of our hearts flow the issues of life.

Denial Has The Power To Defect

There are sly ways that denial slips in to steal, kill and destroy. Let me take a moment and give an example of how this may take place: If your mother and father found out that they were pregnant and declared over the unborn child for months their excitement for the male child, only to find out in the delivery room that their desire did not come to pass, 'it's a girl!", then this is how the unborn child would become confused about her identity. Unknowingly, the parents were in denial and untruth was spoken over the child in the womb. Even though the parents were happy when the child was born, the child picked up on the disappointment of its gender. We need to be careful that our excitement doesn't form denials that defect and influence others in our lives. Choosing the sex of a child is God's decision. Being overly sensitive or extraordinarily excited all of the time is a counterfeit to the true peace of God. You may be in denial of true happiness to the point that you try to make others believe that you are happy. God's peace and joy doesn't have to be put on.

Whatever you put on, you will have to eventually take off.

False intimacy had unconsciously been spoken over the fetus while in the womb; it created a counterfeit relationship. A counterfeit relationship is a relationship based on untruths. She would most likely grow up with gender identity issues. Think about it! For nine months this fetus probably heard from the womb how great it was going to be to have a son, or maybe the plans that were made for the son's life. Maybe when the father or mother addressed the child in the womb, they addressed the child as opposite of the sex that she was.

In this case, now seeking wholeness, she has to revisit the **"forbidden hole of atrocity"** to find her true identity. She has the opportunity as she seeks the truth about her brokenness, to determine that it was not her thoughts convincing her of the unhealthy desires to pursue false intimacy. It was the personality of the generational curse (that came from the untruths spoken over her in the womb) that tried to convince her that it was her own thoughts and feelings. She would actually be convinced that she was born that way! She now needs to become free from the personalities of the generational curse of false intimacy trying to steal her identity. No one has the power to tell you who you are; you must find yourself through Him. You must go back to where you were disillusioned (the forbidden hole of atrocity) and find clarity about your identity.

If your child struggles with untruths about their gender identity, you might want to reflect on if you and/or the father desired a particular sex for the offspring. If you had a role in this, I would go as far as asking the child (even if they are grown) to forgive you for wanting a boy and receiving a girl (or vice versa). Let them know that they were not a mistake and that you love them for who they are.

I ministered this to a lady one time and she agreed that it made real good sense. She admitted to me about having the feelings of wanting a certain sex for a child and receiving the opposite. She went on to say that she didn't think that it had affected her child who was now grown. I then in return asked her, "then why did it come up?" The Holy Spirit was bringing it up to deal with, or she wouldn't have mentioned it in front of the crowd of people. Listen here guys, if we unconsciously try to determine our children's sex, then we too will try to determine their lives. Be real careful not to try to play God. We need to go ahead and deal with the deep issues that we have stuffed so far down in our hearts. When they come up, let them come out.

Dig A Little Deeper In The Well

There are many places in the Bible where people ended up at the well for answers concerning the depths of their delusions. Hagar, the Egyptian handmaiden, in Genesis 21:19 speaks of a miracle produced to save her child named Ishmael.

The well called Beer-lahai-roi.

> Then God opened her eyes and she saw a well of water; and she went and filled the [empty] bottle with water and caused the youth to drink.
>
> Genesis 21:19, AMP

This incident happened when Hagar had given up on life for herself and her offspring. When everything seemingly has ended up as empty as it has ever been, dig a little deeper in the well! When you meet with God at a well, He will open your eyes to receive the water of life. Rebekah met her husband, Isaac, at the well 'Beer-lahai-roi' which means in Hebrew "a well to the Living One Who sees me." If you have been looking for a spouse and it seems hopeless, dig a little deeper in the well!

We also see a metamorphosis take place in the misery of the Samaritan woman that Jesus spoke with in the 4th chapter of John. The guilt and shame that this woman lived with was drowning her daily. If you live with this kind of misery yourself, dig a little deeper in the well! If you think that you have gone as far as you can go and you just can't keep on, dig a little deeper in the well!

May we take this time to epitomize the experience that Moses had at the well he visited while on his fearful excursion? Moses ended up at a well in the middle of his life called nowhere. It is possible that the generational curse of his grandfather, who was Pharaoh, drove him to the well because he was running from him after killing the Egyptian taskmaster. The very decree of murder that his grandfather placed over him when he was a baby began to manifest as part of who he had become. This decree of death was issued over Moses while he was still in the womb. This was not of his own doings, for it was a personality of the generational curse from Pharaoh. If he could have had peace concerning his actions, then this would have proven true, and he wouldn't have had to run in fear. Is it easier to take ownership of this personality when we know that it is not of our own, and end up spending a lifetime of wandering around, or is it easier to stand up and seek the truth and allow the truth to take us into the promise land? Our hunger and thirst for God leads us to the well places in our lives. If you are stuck in the dry places of life, run to the well.

You have to find peace in the well (heart) before you can find peace in the river (life)! The death decree was the very thing that drove Moses' mother to put him in the water and was now driving him out of his homeland. Pharaoh found out about Moses' behavior and desired to kill him (what was new?), which was the very declaration from the beginning. False intimacy cannot be pleased! When you live your life every day trying to please others, this will cause you to one day lose your homeland (joy and peace). Your homeland should be part of your inheritance. Joy and peace should be your daily manna.

Pharaoh raised Moses and taught him about the Egyptian culture, but that was not Moses' destiny. When Moses turned from Pharaoh's way, then Pharaoh wanted him dead. Pharaohs can't be pleased, you either do it their way or not at all! Do you have any Pharaohs in your life? By the power of Jesus Christ and the authority invested in you over two thousand years ago, they must be spiritually dethroned and beheaded, and their unrighteous authority will lose their dominion over your emotions.

WARNING: DO NOT BEHEAD HIM IN THE NATURAL, THIS WILL CAUSE YOU TO GO TO PRISON FOR THE REST OF YOUR LIFE!!!!

The Webster's dictionary defines '*Pharaoh*' as "a tyrant." A '*tyrant*' according to Webster's is "an unrestrained ruler who exercises absolute power oppressively or brutally." Tyrants can also come in female form, better known as Jezebels (I Kings 19). Who is your master? Pharaohs and Jezebels operate under false intimacy, but Jesus Christ operates under true intimacy. Who do you want to serve? We don't have the right to complain about what we tolerate! Other people treat you according to the way that you treat yourself.

Jezebel's and Pharaoh's always want their way.

And if it seems evil to you to serve the Lord, choose for yourselves this day whom you will serve, whether the gods which your fathers served on the other side of the River, or the gods of the Amorites, in whose land you dwell; but as for me and my house, we will serve the Lord.

Joshua 24:15, AMP

As Moses was sitting at the well, he probably thought that his life was over. Maybe he was sitting there contemplating ending his life as he knew it. He may have been confused, lonely, rejected or maybe even felt abandoned. Sound like any well that you have been at lately?

You Die From Drowning , You Live From Drinking

However, his circumstance had to come to an end, before there could ever be a beginning. We have to know that God allows us to visit these well places to give us a drink of His living water, not to drown us. If you are drowning, you've got it all wrong. You're supposed to be drinking.

Suddenly, as he was wallowing in his afflictions, he heard sounds of damsels in distress that accompanied laughs of evil (Ex. 2:16-21). Several scandalous shepherds were after the daughters of his soon-to-be father-in-law. A glimpse of his destiny was being revealed to him as he reached out to save the girls from what the enemy meant for harm. Part of Moses' destiny was to help save others, but what we have to remember is that we can't give what we don't have. You have to be free yourself before you can help set others free. It's a lot easier to help others than to deal with your own issues.

Part of our destiny consists of helping others in distress, but too many times we help others out of our own brokenness, thus postponing our own deliverance. You can't help save someone's life, if you are drowning too. We must help people out of the power that God gives, and not our

202

own; this produces false-burden bearing. '*False burden bearing*' is when you take on other people's problems because you can't seem to be able to do anything about your own. Their problems that you take on become so heavy that you begin to sink as well.

The girls' father heard about this heroic act that helped his daughters and wanted to reward this sojourner for what he had done. An invitation to dinner and a few kind words was all that it took to woo the brokenness of Moses into wanting to be accepted by this family.

Because of our brokenness and neglect of receiving truth (which is denial), we so many times pass up our opportunity to be healed, only to go into more brokenness; yet this feels like what we are supposed to be doing. Moses was on the run from Pharaoh when he stopped by the well to take a drink. Instead of looking down into the well at his own image and seeking the truth about his life, he temporarily quenched his thirst of anxieties and began wondering where his life would go now.

His perception probably prompted him to analyze his abandonment from birth, invalidations from false kinship and the heaviness of hopelessness (not to mention the thought of his grandfather's death threat). The thing that he feared the most had come upon him, having nowhere to go and seemingly no one who cared. And of all things, he is now sitting beside a well out in the middle of life's hardships. I feel as if this was his time and place to gird up and go into the depths of his brokenness and get over himself. Even though he had helped the girls and began to see some of his destiny, he probably still had a great struggle on his hands emotionally because of the issues of his past life.

When we are at the place that we are about to get over ourselves, **any offer of acceptance will invite us to procrastinate our deliverance**. Everything was seemingly great when Jethro, (the father of the girls who Moses saved), offered his daughter's hand in marriage as reward for his bravery. Any acceptance and affection, after a lifetime of no acceptance and affection, is better than nothing. Just for the record, if you fall prey to this, you will end up investing forty more years tending to someone else's business. The very thing that you won't deal with now, will deal with you later and derail you from God's promises. This is when Moses found himself on the backside of Horeb tending to his father-in-law's flock.

A good indication that you are called is the very fact that what you have been through didn't kill you. You remember that motto, *"What doesn't kill you, will only make you stronger?"* This is a statement from our society that has caused us to agree with negative happenings to the point that at least we are not dead from them. In all actuality, we unconsciously blame God for the things that come to us that almost kill us, only to make us stronger. How's that working for us? If it doesn't kill us, but leaves us stronger (and we're almost dead), that's insane. We must know that it is God's mercy that didn't allow that thing to kill us, and we are to give glory where glory is due. Because you are chosen and have a call on your life is the real reason things come to knock you out before your time. I re-wrote this motto last summer after I had my experience at the well. Here it goes:

"What Doesn't Kill You, Just Doesn't!"

Little children, you are of God [you belong to Him] and have [already] defeated and overcome them [the agents of the antichrist], because He Who lives in you is greater (mightier) than he who is in the world.

1 John 4:4, AMP

Jesus told the woman at the well in John 4:14 AMP, *"But whoever takes a drink of the water that I will give him shall never, no never, be thirsty any more. But the water that I will give him shall become a spring of water welling up (flowing, bubbling) [continually] within him unto (into, for) eternal life."* In order to be filled up, we must first become whole to hold the power of His healing. Paul said this best when he described his ministering to the people as being a drink offering being poured out before them. The Bible also says in John 7:38 AMP, *"He who believes in Me, [who cleaves to and trusts in and relies on Me] as the Scripture has said, From his innermost being shall flow [continuously] springs and rivers of living water."*

I have a friend who sings a song, "Knee deep in the river and dying of thirst." Won't you let Jesus take you to that well of living waters today where you will never thirst again? Will you give the Master permission today to take you to the depths of your distresses, and set you free from yourself? God desires to save you from drowning and give you a drink of His goodness. Will we allow God's glory to change our emptiness like He did for Hagar, opening our eyes to His provisions? (Genesis 21:19) You may say that you don't have a well to have this experience at. Neither did Hagar, but when God opened her eyes, a well appeared and saved her and her offspring from perishing. Again, our stuff, our brokenness, will keep us and our children from life. Jesus came that "no one should perish, but have eternal life" (John 3:16). He will make a way where there seems to be no way.

He is the Way Maker!

Can we determine this day that no one else is our enemy? Have we attacked ourselves to the point of destruction? Hagar's enemy (Sarah) pushed her into the wilderness, but Hagar's self-pity was going to be the cause of her generational extinction. Quit blaming others (victimization) for pushing you around, and take action for yourself to come out from where you have been traumatized. When you have a victory mentality, then you can appreciate when the enemy pushes you. He thinks that he is pushing you further into the wilderness. In all actuality, he is pushing you closer to the throne of God. Today can be your very own well experience. Right now, where you sit, God can begin this process of making you whole.

Can we admit today that no one else is our enemy and take accountability?

May we just stop right here and pray?

My Dear Savior and Friend,

Jesus, I love You so, and I thank You for the revelation that You have given me as I have read this book and understand that "Yea though I have walked through the valley (my life) of the shadow of death, I <u>fear</u> no evil." Lord, I understand that the valley is my journey and that I do not have to be afraid of things that fall upon me as a shadow of death. You are my rod and my staff, and You comfort me all the days of my life. Just as the table has been prepared before me in the presence of mine enemies, I will eat and be satisfied in Your presence alone. I will eat of your goodness and rest in Your peaceful purpose for my life here. I repent for being my own enemy and ask that You forgive me for the way fear, doubt and unbelief have kept me from Your provisions, and I also forgive myself. May my life hold an eternal ingredient of Your heavenly banquet menu that will be served at the great wedding feast. You alone are worthy of all my praise. As I continue what you have started, may the light of Your glory forever shine through me to touch the world. In Jesus' Name.

NOTES

CHAPTER 12

FOR THE DEEP IS WELL

The very first thing that I acknowledged about the well the day I "*got over myself*" was how deep the well was. I never knew that the glory of God was deeper and more powerful then anything thing I had ever experienced. I didn't know how deep my wounds were from the false intimacy that clouded my perception. Nor did I realize the depths of generational curses that caused afflictions to be deep rooted within my family tree.

The Greek/Hebrew meaning of '*deep*' is "treacherous; taking from a primary root word that means to cover (with a garment); to act covertly." The word '*treacherous*' in Webster's dictionary is defined as "likely to betray trust; UNRELIABLE." The word '*covertly*' is defined by Webster's as being "a hidden place, SHELTER; not openly shown or veiled."

Genesis 1 says, *"In the beginning, God created the heaven and earth. And the earth was without form, and void; and darkness was upon the face of the deep. And the spirit of God moved upon the face of the waters. The earth was without form."* **'*Form*'** is "a shape, vessel or something that needs a purpose, just as a vat is to wine." Wine could not be contained if it were not for the vat and vice versa. The vat would have no purpose without the wine. The earth was also '*void*' meaning "vacant, deserted, not inhabited, useless or empty," all according to Webster's dictionary. This place called earth was created by God as an empty, useless vessel that needed a purpose (God), just as we are an earthen vessel that is also in need of God. Without Him, we have no purpose.

He is our purpose!

In other words, God created the earth which was without form, and you may ask the question, "How can God create something, and it be void and without form?" He is the creator of all things; so therefore, He can do whatever He wills. We always assume (maybe it's the way we were taught to believe) that God is so sovereign, that nothing happens without His allowance of the happening. This is not true. Don't get me wrong or put words in my mouth concerning this, GOD IS SOVEREIGN. But, we haven't been taught right about the sovereignty of God, or we would not unrighteously blame Him for things that go wrong.

If I tell my kids not to play in the road, and they disobey me, and they eventually get hit by a car, did I allow this to happen? No! We get hurt a lot of times by the things in which we have become rebellious to!!! We end up blaming God when we get hurt (or when others hurt us), because we assume that God allowed it to happen. Our assumptions are not God's allowances! This is the deception that caused Adam to blame God for giving him the woman that offered him the fruit. Wake up Church, God is not the one that needs to be blamed. The Word of God says that if God be for us then who can be against us (Romans 8:31). God is not sitting back waiting for us to fall where He can say, "I told you so." He is ready and willing to help us and keep us from falling, if we don't unrighteously blame Him for things that happen to us because of the enemy. Does this sound familiar?

In what ways have we disobeyed God and ended up emptied by our own ignorance. We must rearrange our arrogant attitudes and repent for the assumptions that we have accused God with. Our spiritually inheritance is already accounted for and must now be accepted.

Our Assumptions Are Not God's Allowances

You know what assumptions make you. We have to learn to be the head and not the rear end! God's wisdom is available to us for guidance, but unless we apply it, it is formless. He needs a vat (earthen vessel) for His heavenly wine (power) to reside in, in order for us to not only help ourselves stay out of unsafe places, but also to help others. Will you allow me to share a bit more of this revelation with you?

Then God said, *"Let there be light."* It is the light of God's glory that penetrates the deepest parts of our being and creates purpose that explores our destiny. In other words, the darkness that is within our hearts (that has been hidden because of our brokenness) is bombarded with the glory light of God and exposes its hidden agendas and delivers us to our destiny. Without our destiny, we would be just like the earth without purpose. The earth was just a dry place that God created that would be used to hold His glory.

> For the earth shall be filled with the knowledge of the glory of the Lord, as the waters cover the sea.
>
> Habakkuk 2:14, KJV

We are His glory in action, and we are also covering the earth as His glory uncovers us from the treacherous things that have tried to keep us veiled from our destiny. A well is no good if it has been covered and hidden. When I went to the well that day on my great-grandfather's farm, little did I know that God would give me the revelation to uncover it in the natural. The lady who tended the orchards told me that in the twenty years she had worked there, she never knew that the well was there. It was covered up with years of vine growth that hid it from the world.

In the supernatural, my obedience to a God I have never seen before uncovered me from the hidden curses that had veiled me from my destiny, like the vines had veiled the well. Our destiny is to operate under the glory! If you're covered with the vines of your past, then you remain hidden from your destiny. The greater glory comes as we acknowledge Him in all of His glory, and then more is revealed. He saw the light and said, *"This is good."* God acknowledged Himself, and that brought forth His greater glory.

We must seek the open door that has been made available to us to receive a new heart; as David prayed, *"Lord, create in me a clean heart"* *(Ps. 51:10).* We have veiled our hearts to the point that things get stuck in them that never should have been experienced. Anything that has been stopped up by interruptions becomes stagnated to the point that no one wants to partake of it. Once our hearts become dammed up, this disables the flow of God's power to set us free. God wants to heal our hearts because His Word says, *"Out of the abundance of a man's heart his mouth will speak" (Matt. 12:34).* Our hearts become stopped up with things such as unforgiveness and bitterness, and then our mouths compliment what's keeping our hearts out of overflow.

'Overflow' is when our bellies gush forth the power (water) of the Spirit of God via the heart that will cause the mouth to tell of His goodness. If your mouth is not lining up with the power of the Holy Spirit of God, you might want to consider cleaning out your heart. This will enable the power from your belly to spring forth like water gushing up through your very being.

Remember, Jesus told the woman at the well, *"Whosoever drinketh of the water that I shall give him shall never thirst; but the water that I shall give him shall be in him a well of water springing up into everlasting life" (John 4:14 KJV).* She then dropped her water pot, and ran off to tell the others of His goodness. Her heart was cleansed as the water that she partook of gushed out of her belly, causing her to face the community in humility, and share what she had received from Jesus.

When you are in overflow, the very power of God forces you to run towards what you normally dread with a voice of triumph. You are the well! Her insecurities of her past had dammed up her heart, and when she forgave herself at the well, she was set free from herself to the point that she began evangelizing the truth. She had to drop her brokenness, what she had always depended upon to contain the water. Her brokenness had to be traded in before the new wine could come forth (wine and water are symbolic of the spirit and power of God).

The new wine of God will intoxicate you to the point that you no longer care what others say about you. You receive what He says about you as truth, and that in return sets you free from yourself. She asked Jesus was He greater than her ancestor Jacob who gave her the well (John 4:12). In other words, the curse that was on her life was manifesting and prompted her to ask Jesus if He was greater than the curse. The end of the story reveals the greater power. Don't let the curse that is on your life convince you that Jesus' power is not great enough to set you free.

How to Be Free From Me

The law of reflection in the natural consists of seeing opposite of truth, which is deception. I am a hair designer, and my clients often ask me if I am left-handed. It's actually funny because when I tell them that I'm not, they look confused. In the mirror, everything is opposite to that in the natural. Webster's dictionary defines the word 'reflection' as "an image given back by a reflecting surface." The day I looked into the well and the Lord asked me what did I see, all I saw was my boring reflection in the water at the bottom of the well.

He said when He looked in the water, *"Let there be light,"* and there was light, and He said, that it was good. He saw Himself in His own reflection; so therefore, light complimented light, which made it become greater. The glory is God reflecting Himself in you and as it comes forth, it creates the greater glory.

That day at the well, when I looked in the water and didn't see myself as light (as He sees me) I automatically said, "This is not good!" (What do you say when you look in your mirror?) This was opposite to how He saw me. I saw myself how my brokenness had taught me to see myself, which now I know is deception. It is the opposite of how God sees me. When we can learn to get over ourselves and acknowledge the glory of God that is in us, then we will see the greater glory. It pleases God when we look at ourselves and see Him!

The enemy's job is to distort our vision of ourselves, because if we can't see ourselves as God sees us, then our chances of thriving here on earth are slim to none. God doesn't want us just to survive; He wants us to thrive and prosper. God wants us to see ourselves as the conquerors that we are, instead of playing the role of a victim our whole lives.

If we don't stand for the truth, we will fall for anything. If you don't see yourself as God sees you, then you will eventually fall prey to seeing yourself as satan sees you. Not only will you believe the lies that he repetitiously whispers to you, you will also conform to the lifestyle of what he says about you.

This book is not for Sally Sue that thinks she's got it all together and never misses a church service. This book is for the man or woman who knows that there is more around the corner than just what religion has to offer. Religion will not set you free from yourself; it will only justify and prolong your agony of procrastination of getting set free.

> That He might present it to Himself a glorious church, not having spot, or wrinkle, or any such thing; but that it should be holy and without blemish.

> Ephesians 5:27, KJV

Religion will not set you free from yourself!

Without Spot Blemish Or Wrinkle

I had a vision one time of going down the altar as a bride, and all that I saw at the end of the aisle was a purple cloth waving as if it were alive. I heard the voice of God say, *"Come to the cloth."* There was a crowd of people on both sides of me. Hesitantly I staggered, longing to arrive at the end of the altar, but also fearing the gaze of so many others awaiting my performance.

I heard the Lord again say, *"Come to the cloth."* Without further ado, I held my head high and pranced towards the sound of His presence. Arriving at the cloth, I heard Him say, *"You made it without spot, blemish, or wrinkle; you have finally made it."* I was somewhat relieved at the fact that I did make it, but the part about being without spot, blemish, or wrinkle made no sense to me. The Lord explained to me that the thoughts and judgments of other people were what stained my perception of myself, but He sees me without spot, blemish, or wrinkle. He sees me through His eyes, not the eyes of others. Man looks upon the outward appearance, but God looks upon the heart.

I made it through the sea of people to the altar of His presence, only to find the answers to my lifelong quest. I had been covering myself with the treacherous garments of what others taught me, and/or thought of me; but in truth, I was created to be covered by His garments of Royalty. The purple cloth was symbolic of royalty, and it is alive and waiting to be worn. We must burst through the thoughts and impressions of all others to get to Him to truly see ourselves as He sees us.

Almost a year later, I was preaching at a conference in Foley, Alabama, when a lady came up to me and said that God told her to give me a gift. I had never met this woman before. When she revealed what the gift was, it was the same purple garment that I saw waving at the altar in the vision. God will always confirm Himself to His people!

Man looks upon the outward appearance but God looks on the heart.

Back to the creation of the earth. The face of the deep was covered with the waters of God's glory (remember the glory is in the water). Apparently, His glory saw a need and filled the need. This is what the glory does; it sees a need and then comes to fill the need as we acknowledge it as our provision. This is what we refer to as the "deep calling the deep." God's glory has already filled the depths of our soul; we just have to acknowledge it before we realize that His glory has already done for us all that we have need of.

He then hovered over the water and saw His reflection and said, *"Let there be light"* and there was light and He said, *"This is good."* We must allow God's Spirit to hover over the places within us that, in all actuality, He has already filled. He wants an opportunity to see Himself within us, so we must realize our need for Him to bring forth completion.

We first have to see ourselves as He sees us to recognize it as being Him within us. If we continuously look through our natural eyes, we will look at ourselves through our brokenness. But if we deal with our stuff and get over ourselves, then and only then, are we able to see ourselves as He does. When we are made whole, we can see ourselves as He does, and then we will be able to say, "This is GOOD" about ourselves. He sees Himself within us and calls it GOOD. This will consist of changing positions in the natural in order to get over ourselves!

A Christian Cast Away

I had become a Christian castaway! I had cast myself away (like Jonah), not giving myself a chance to be my own purpose. Jonah didn't fear Ninevah, he feared himself! I couldn't find my purpose because that consisted of accepting myself.

The Webster's dictionary defines 'castaway' as REJECTED. I had rejected myself, and in return assumed others would as well. *"As a man thinketh in his heart, so is he."* As long as we reject ourselves, we can't receive others' acceptance.

A castaway on a ship seeks to find land, a new beginning, a new start in life, a place of freedom. First, I had to cut myself loose from the anchor of unforgiveness that was holding me down, and then throw away the oars of abandonment that steered me in the wrong direction. I wanted to find land, land that was healed and made whole.

The Lord says in His Word in 2 Chronicles 7:14, (KJV), *"If My people which are called by My name, shall humble themselves, and pray, and seek my face, and turn from their wicked ways; then will I hear from heaven, and will forgive their sin, and will heal their land."* I asked the Lord to explain to me what "LAND" was in this passage of scripture. He said that *"land"* was the thirty percent uncovered that He desired to cover with His glory for our completion.

The earth is made up of seventy percent water and thirty percent land. Think it not strange that our bodies are also made up of seventy percent water! God's Spirit, which is symbolized as water, covers seventy percent of our bodies, just as seventy percent of the earth is covered. In other words, His Spirit has covered the depths of who we are. All we have to be concerned about is the remaining uncovered thirty percent, which is land. We are not as bad off as the enemy has tried to convince us that we are!

The Word of God says that we are made up of three things: body, soul and spirit. Our spirit man is the seventy percent that is covered. You don't have to worry about your spirit man! He is fine; He can't be sick. He doesn't need chemotherapy or three meals a day. Stop worrying about your spirit man.

People often say that they feel things in their spirit man, but so often what they feel doesn't line up with the truth. The truth is that we feel with our emotions, which are a component of our soul. What we have

215

need of is the discernment of God to set us free from feelings that confuse our minds into thinking that we are worse off than even God Himself knows. God knows exactly how bad off we are. This is why He sent His only begotten Son and filled the deepest, darkest places within us and brought forth light (life).

Here is the kicker!!!! The thirty percent that remains uncovered by His Spirit is the land part that He wants to heal, according to 2 Chronicles 7:14. The land consists of thirty percent that our free will affects (fifteen percent soul and fifteen percent body).

15% Soul   (Mind, Will & Emotions)
15% Body   (Physical Make-up)
70% Spirit (Spirit Man)

_____

100% WHOLE IN JESUS NAME!

If we take care of our soul, the chances of our bodies being healed are greater, because it is negative emotions that bring forth death to our bodies. For example, the Word of God says that *"Envy and jealousy are the rottenness of thy bones" (Prov. 14:30)*. When we repent of envy and jealousy (which are feelings), then repentance will usher in healing, and your body will have a greater chance of being healed of things such as osteoporosis, arthritis and other afflictions. If we will repent and get our emotions under control, then healing can come forth and make us whole. To recap, seventy percent of our being is spirit, (our spirit man doesn't need anything) fifteen percent soul, (mind, will and emotions), and fifteen percent body.

People, we can be made WHOLE!

Now, let me explain something to you. One of the first questions that God had for Adam was, *"Who told you that you were naked?" (Gen.3:11)* In other words, who told you how to have shame? Who told you how to blame others? Who told you how to cover up your sin? The

Lord knows all things, but He wanted to enlighten Adam on the fact of false covering. The fig leaves were not supposed to cover man. God's glory was supposed to cover man. God's glory is the ultimate covering for man. Therefore, if we have false coverings upon us, we must first realize this, and get out from under anything that would keep us from being made whole. Remember, the spirit only covers seventy percent, and the rest is up to us and our free will to allow the glory to uncover that which has been covered by the counterfeit. We must remove all counterfeit coverings in order to get set,

"BUTT NAKED FREE."

And not a creature exists that is concealed from His sight, but all things are open *and* exposed, naked *and* defenseless to the eyes of Him with Whom we have to do.

Hebrews 4:13, AMP

I was scheduled to speak on the East Coast once, when my mother asked me what I was going to be teaching on. I told her that the Lord told me to teach His people how to get set "BUTT NAKED FREE." This is God's original intention for His creation to be naked before Him in all of our humanistic humilities. In what ways have we covered ourselves with the counterfeit and called it the real thing?

I was ministering to a man one time, and he was offended when I told him that what he called peace was the counterfeit, because when he told me that he had peace, it was in a very harsh tone. I simply said, *"You do not have the true peace of God,"* and he screamed back to me, *"YES I DO."* I in return said, *"Then why are you screaming?"* Like I said earlier, in what ways have we covered ourselves up with the counterfeit and called it God? Who told us that we were naked?

We were made for peace. When we don't have it and we cover ourselves up with the counterfeit, it makes us mad when others figure us out. This man who said that he had peace was mad because he knew that he didn't, and he really got mad with me when I told him that he didn't. He wanted peace! I don't know a human being alive that doesn't want peace. We get mad at ourselves, others and God when we don't have something that we were created to carry. So therefore, we have to figure out what it is that has kept us from operating in all that God has for us for such a time as this.

It is our fears that keep us from exploring the places that remain hidden, or maybe fears that others have taught us. The things that have come against us that have kept us out of our destiny, are the very things that we need to overcome. We must uncover ourselves, which makes us available for a new heart; and when we receive that new heart, then a door opens for us to walk into the supernatural. When we walk in the supernatural, we see things as they were intended to be seen.

The revelation of God reveals the intentions of God.

We must also be aware that we are no longer the victim. This is now our time of victory to go in and get what the enemy has taken from us for so long. True Intimacy has prepared a way before us to walk into and become that true bride that we have so longed and desired to be. We have to allow renovation to come to our lives in order to see restoration.

Remember, we must tear out the old to make room for the new. This consists of areas of desolation that invites His presence always, so be prepared to conquer your feelings of loneliness. We must know the definition of True Intimacy in order to operate in the potential of its power. We also have to be aware of the deception that has formed the foundation of False Intimacy where we will never be fooled again to the point of destruction.

Validation desires to overthrow and overtake any and all areas of invalidation, so we can be that new creation that He desires for us to be. It is not too late for you, my friend. Now is your time to be dismissed from the generational curses that have been hidden that held your families in captivity for generations. The glory of God brought forth revelation for such a time as this to insure your deliverance. Come out of the place of drought and denial and go forth now into the place that the waters never run dry. The enemy has tried for years to convince you that you were stuck in the deserted dry places of life. This is what the Word of God says about you:

> Behold, I will do a new thing; now it shall spring forth; shall ye not know it? I will even make a way in the wilderness, and rivers in the desert.
>
> Isaiah 43:19, KJV

You are the well...
And you are well, my friend!!!

For the deep calleth the deep, and so too,
The God of all Glory
Calleth you forth now
To be everything that you always knew
you could be.

SHALOM.

We invite you to contact us

Rebecca L. King
Harvest Time Ministries
108 W. Washington Ave.
Nashville, Ga 31639

Visit our website for videos, cd's,
books and ebooks.

http://www.rebeccakingministries.com

or email us

mystoryforhisglory@yahoo.com

Made in the USA
Middletown, DE
26 September 2015